Violence and responsibility

Violence
and responsibility

John Harris

Routledge & Kegan Paul
London, Boston and Henley

First published in 1980
by Routledge & Kegan Paul Ltd
39 Store Street, London WC1E 7DD,
9 Park Street, Boston, Mass. 02108 USA and
Broadway House, Newtown Road,
Henley-on-Thames, Oxon RG9 1EN
Set in 11/12 IBM Press Roman by Columns
and printed in Great Britain by
Redwood Burn Ltd
Trowbridge & Esher
© John Harris, 1980

British Library Cataloguing in Publication Data

Harris, John

Violence and responsibility.
1. Violence   2. Responsibility
I. Title
301.6'33'01   BF575.A3   79 41531

ISBN 0 7100 0448 6

Contents

Acknowledgments

The ideas discussed in this book have so dominated my
thoughts for a number of years that I have plagued almost
everyone I've met with some aspect of them. The result has
been that I have received more help than I can remember
let alone acknowledge. I have, however, at various times
received detailed comments from Jonathan Glover, Mike
Inwood, Alan Montefiore, Alan Ryan, Anne Seller and Vicky
Tagart to all of whom I am very much indebted.

Thanks are also due to the editors of *Philosophy and
Public Affairs*, *Philosophy* and the *Philosophical Quarterly*,
for helping me to clarify some of the ideas in Chapters 2,
3, 5 and 7.

I am grateful to Professor Kenneth Walton of Birmingham
University Medical School for saving me from a number of
errors in the discussion of transplantation and coronary care.

My DPhil examiners at Oxford, Derek Parfit and James
Griffin went carefully through an earlier draft and provided
valuable corrections and criticism, and I have taken Ted
Honderich's generous advice on a number of points.

Jill Engelhart, Nick Stanley and Sita Williams have helped
me in that most valuable of ways, with moral support.

Finally, my greatest debt by far is to Ronald Dworkin who
has discussed almost every aspect of this book with me and
from whose detailed criticism and continued encouragement
I have greatly benefited.

if a man could write a book on
Ethics which really was a book
on Ethics, this book would,
with an explosion, destroy all
the other books in the world.

Ludwig Wittgenstein '*A Lecture on Ethics*'

Chapter 1

Humans and persons

If we are responsible for harm which we could have prevented and if we believe that we should not harm others, we will find ourselves committed to a morality which challenges many of our basic beliefs and one which makes disturbing demands. I shall argue that we are indeed responsible for the harm we could have prevented and explore the effect of this conclusion on a morality which makes fundamental the belief that we ought not to harm others if we can possibly avoid it. This belief is very widely if not universally held, it has a fundamental place in most moralities including our own, and it is, therefore, of some importance to be clear about just what it entails. Since those fates that people consider to be worse than death are rare, the principle that heads the list of those which are expressions of this belief, is the absolute prohibition of killing. For this reason we shall often concentrate on death as the most extreme form of harm.

There are two ways in which we inflict harm on our fellows. I am interested particularly in one of these, one which although it has a very long history, has never played a part commensurate with its importance in our moral thinking. One way of inflicting harm on others is to do something which results in their being harmed; the other, is to fail to do something the consequence of which is that they are harmed, in short, to fail to prevent harm. This distinction can be characterised in a number of ways: sometimes as a distinction between acts and omissions, or between positive and negative acts, between harming and failing to help or, where life and death are at issue, as a distinction between killing and letting die.

We have, then, two ways of determining the state of any

world in which we are able to intervene. One is to intervene and to change the state of that world, the other is to refrain from intervention and to leave everything as it is. This page can stand for a world in which you are able to intervene. You have two ways of determining how this world will be, one is by leaving it as it is, the other by changing it, writing in the margins, striking out remarks with which you disagree, or reducing the entire world to ashes. Whatever you decide the decision is yours and yours the responsibility.

For those who have allowed our world to survive: it is the omissions, the failures to save, the negative actions which result in harm to persons, that I wish to examine here. I am going to concentrate exclusively on this dimension of the harm we inflict on one another for a number of reasons: because it is the most problematic, because if we are consistently to follow the principle that we should not harm others, it is the avoidance of this sort of harm that is most difficult to reconcile with our other moral beliefs, because it has until recently been largely neglected by moral philosophy and lastly and most important, because I believe that the neglect of this dimension of harm has been responsible for untold misery in the world.

The formulation of the distinction between acts and omissions that I prefer is that between *positive actions* and *negative actions*, for my concern is to sensitise people to what they are *doing* to each other. This will strike some people as a highly controversial way of putting the point but I hope to justify it in the course of this essay.

Much of the harm which results from our negative actions can, I believe, be directly attributed to the wide acceptance of the view that the distinction between positive and negative actions marks a distinction both in the causal efficacy of what we do, and in its moral significance. Those who accept this distinction hold that it is always worse to cause harm or death positively rather than negatively and, often, that the causal connection between an act and its consequences is necessarily somehow *closer* than that between an omission and its consequences.

There is perhaps a difficulty about drawing this distinction at all since it is always possible to re-formulate any action description or any omission description so that each becomes the other. Although I fail to save you I am still doing *something* instead, and if your death is a consequence of my failure to save you, it is a consequence of whatever else I do when I could be saving you, more tortuously: if I shoot you, your death is a consequence of my failure not to shoot. Despite these rather devious locutions, the distinction between acts and omissions is an obvious enough one and I will continue to use it.

The belief that we should not harm others is sometimes expressed in terms of rights. We talk of the right to life and the right not to be killed. I shall here avoid talk of rights for I am not concerned with what rights people happen to have, but with what we ought to do if we believe that we should not harm others. It may be that in the light of our deliberations we would wish to change our system of rights, or abandon it, or understand it differently. But I will not draw these conclusions specifically.

The argument to the effect that we are responsible for the harm we could have prevented and the exploration of the consequences of this conclusion for our morality, will run concurrently throughout this essay. This method of proceeding is dictated by the nature of the enquiry; for showing just how we are equally responsible for what we do and for what we fail to prevent, and meeting objections to this view, itself reveals the ways in which our morality is affected by it.

For our purposes it is not important to decide precisely what is and what is not to count as harm. It is, however, tempting to believe that there are a number[1] of natural shocks and disasters that flesh is heir to. One of the purposes of this essay is to modify our conception of how many of the disasters that so often befall us are inevitable, and how many are, so to speak, man-made. I shall, therefore, assume that we are fairly good at recognising a disaster when we encounter it and concentrate on re-assessing the proportion of them for which we are responsible, and on looking at some of the consequences of this re-assessment.

But who are *we*? If we believe that we should not harm others if we can avoid doing so, it does very much matter, especially to them, who is to be included. Clearly, we usually have in mind here other people, and this is most often taken simply to mean other human beings; but we need a more sophisticated concept of the person than one which confines its use unproblematically and parochially to the human species.

We might, for example, want to know whether a particularly sophisticated machine, a type of computer perhaps, had acquired personality, had become a person, or whether a human being, heavily patched up with mechanical bits and pieces, had remained one. It is also, of course, a real question as to whether there are persons on other planets.

Treating these as real and problematic issues has important consequences. If we consider that feature which has perhaps the clearest claim to being the most significant among any that would lead us to call something a person, namely language (and the sorts of thinking which language makes possible)[2], then these consequences are already with us. Much work has been done recently towards the education of a number of animals, and some chimpanzees have been taught quite rich forms of language.[3] In view of this we will have to take seriously not the issue of animals' rights, but of full rights for articulate animals.

But even if we feel lazy about recognising the status of chimpanzees as fully fledged persons on the basis of a few cases of proven capacity to learn language, there are possible circumstances that would concern us more closely.

Fred Hoyle wrote about one such possibility in his science fiction novel *The Black Cloud*. The story so far: a huge cloud of gases has descended on our solar system and now blocks out the sun threatening to cool the earth to extinction. Scientists have discovered that it must be a vast brain possessing immense intelligence and comparatively unlimited powers.[4] They try to communicate with it in the hope of persuading it to go away. The method is to bombard it with radio and television signals supposing that it will be able to learn our language, if we give it enough information, much more quickly than we could possibly learn its own. We drop in on two scientists discussing whether their plan has any hope of success. Now read on. . . .[5]

'But seriously, do you think this communication business will work?'

'I very much hope so, it's quite crucial that it should.'

'Why do you say that?'

'Think of the disasters the Earth has suffered so far, without the Cloud taking any purposive steps against us. A bit of reflection from its surface nearly roasted us. A short obscuration of the sun nearly froze us. If the merest tiny fraction of the energy controlled by the Cloud should be directed against us we should be wiped out, every plant and animal.'

'But why should that happen?'

'How can you tell? Do you think of the tiny beetle or the ant that you crush under your foot on an afternoon's walk? One of those gas bullets that hit the moon three months ago would finish us. Sooner or later the Cloud will probably let fly with some more of 'em. Or we might be electrocuted in some monstrous discharge.'

'Could the Cloud really do that?'

'Easily, the energy that it controls is simply enormous. If we can get some sort of message across, then perhaps the Cloud will take the trouble to avoid crushing us under its foot.'

'But why should it bother?'

'Well, if a beetle were to say to you, "Please Miss Halsey, will you avoid treading here, otherwise I shall be crushed", wouldn't you be willing to move your foot a trifle?'

Here is a case where we might have a tremendous interest in being recognised as persons ourselves. So the concept of a person which may be broadened in one direction to include articulate animals and machines may from another direction be broadened to include ourselves!

Having put ourselves as persons into some sort of perspective I intend now to concentrate on human persons. But we should just note that beings that do not count as persons do not therefore count for nothing. All questions as to how non-persons are to be treated must be decided on their merits. Animals have found powerful champions recently with arguments that will prove hard to answer,[6] and the human foetus, if not a person is not, for that reason at any rate, fair game.

The principle with which this work is concerned, that we should not harm others if we can avoid it, can of course be applied to all other creatures, although I shall not do so.

I have said that we will often concentrate on killing as the most extreme form of harm, but there are some cases where killing others may be considered to benefit them. There are three sorts of case that arise here. The first two concern people whose lives are, or are about to become, so dreadful that we judge death to be preferable to living under those conditions. The cases are of those who

1   consequently wish to die or,
2   nonetheless wish to go on living.

The other case concerns those whose lives we cannot think are so bad that death would be preferable but who

3   nonetheless wish to die.

I shall assume that it is sensible to say that in case 1 we and they agree that to kill them would not be to harm them but would rather benefit them, and that in cases 2 and 3 we and they disagree about just this point.

Case 1 then does not present problems to people who believe that they should not harm others if they can help it, for here all are agreed that we would be harming people if we compelled them to go on living.

Case 2 involves either disagreement as to whether continuing alive is a fate worse than death[7], or agreement that it is, but a wish to experience a fate worse than death. Now, to deny people the direction of their own lives, to deprive them of the power of choice over their own destiny, in short, to treat them as incompetent to run their own lives as they choose, is to offer them the most profound of insults. It may also lead to the most acute frustration and the sense that life has lost its meaning and importance. Autonomy has a very special role. People have been prepared to lay down their lives in order to win autonomy with respect to quite minor sorts of decisions. Many things that we would find delightful if we had chosen them for ourselves, lose all their charm when they are seen to have been chosen for us by others. So to deny people autonomy is to do them a very fundamental sort of harm. Our sense of ourselves as autonomous beings so colours the whole conduct of our lives that it is difficult to know what weight to give it. A life that seems thoroughly rich and worthwhile may be so only on the assumption that we wish to live it; if we are *condemned* to live it, it may be worthless to us.

Even in the timeless case of soldiers forced to abandon a wounded comrade in the face of an advancing and exceptionally cruel enemy, at whose hands his fate will almost certainly be unspeakable, there does seem to be something wrong with killing the wounded soldier against his will. Sure, his fate will be worse than death, and sure *we* would prefer to die now rather than live a little longer and then die under torture. But so long as the wounded soldier does not wish to die now, so long as he chooses to fall into the hands of the enemy, there does seem to be something wrong with killing him.

If we think so, we will also have to allow the autonomous choice of those in case 3, whose lives are worth living but who nonetheless wish to die. This is perhaps the usual case where we encounter attempted suicide. It is rare for those who know in detail about the lives of those who have tried to kill themselves to say, 'yes, if I had your life to lead I would prefer to be dead'. They think that if the attempted suicides had a proper perspective it would not seem to them that life was not worth living, or that they would see this feeling as transitory and so see the sense of hanging on until things improved. But so long as someone has decided sincerely and soberly that they would prefer to be dead, then it does seem outrageous for us to condemn them to live lives that we, not they, judge to be worth living; not because we are *wrong* about their lives, we may not be, not because they know better, they may not, but because it's *their lives*.

Is the reason that we must respect autonomy then because to fail to do so is to harm others more than does whatever it is that we wish to prevent them doing to themselves? We could make this a definition, but it does not seem to be true. We can imagine someone sincerely wishing to die *because* this is the worst possible thing that could happen to him. Whatever the reason for the sacrifice, it *is* a sacrifice. The agony of being frustrated in making the sacrifice, exquisite though it might be, is less than that of an untimely death.

So, although the denial of autonomy is a harm it is by no means necessarily the worst harm that can befall us. How important it is is difficult to say. Is it always so important as to make us judge that we should respect the wishes of those in cases 2 and 3? I think it is but I can understand the views of those who do not.

In any event we must, I think, see the belief that we should not harm others as expressive of concern for those others — to believe that we should not harm them is to care about *them*. This involves us in not merely giving great weight to the things about them that matter to us, but in accepting the importance of the things that matter to them. This is the point at which concern becomes also respect, where what matters is not simply other people's needs but also their wants,[8] where we value not only their lives but their autonomy. This sense of the point of our principles can be important, as we will see in Chapter 7.

I have digressed far enough to indicate, if not to argue for, my belief that our morality must apply at the very least to all persons and not simply to all humans; and that we must take a wide view of what it is to do one another harm. All of this is just for the record, since I am now going to write for those who already believe that we should not harm others, whoever the others are, and try to show just how demanding a principle this is.

I do not, of course, suppose that this is the only or even the most fundamental principle of morality. It is, however, fortunately widely held and widely accepted as of great importance. I want to build on this acceptance and examine the consequent view of both our agency and our responsibility.

We start in perhaps a surprising place with the concept of violence. This has both 'historical' and theoretical justifications which need explaining. When, a number of years ago, I first became interested in violence as a philosophical problem, I rapidly became convinced that proponents of what is often called 'quiet violence' or 'the violence of normal times' were not simply conceptually confused as their opponents usually insisted, but were trying to express something that they saw as a truth about our relationships with each other. This idea of quiet violence we shall shortly be examining more closely, but it is contrasted with the violence of assault and battery and is simply the bringing about of harm by neglect or omission. I found that it was impossible to give a coherent account of the structure of this view without a theory of negative actions and so began to investigate this vexed question. It was these investigations which forced on me the conclusion which is the subject of this essay, that there can be no moral difference between positive and negative actions with the same consequences. This conclusion I shall from time to time refer to as 'the negative actions thesis'. It is because I now see the central argument of this essay in terms of our violence to one another that we will begin by examining the concept of violence.

Chapter 2

A defence of non–'violent' violence

Few categories of conduct evoke more concern than 'violence'. Social critics equate violence with decay, statesmen deplore its prevalence, and unprecedented resources are marshalled to combat it. Everyone agrees that we are a violent people. The mass media are presumed suffused with cruelty, and they in turn claim that the masses have a propensity for gore. We are told that violence lurks within us, that we dote on it, wallow in it, and that we must exert enormous effort to suppress it.

During the crises that follow assassinations and riots, speculation about violence reaches feverish proportions. Violence becomes the monomania of the press, the core substance of politics, the mainstay of the cocktail party, and the obsession of the public. Violence is promiscuously viewed, and it is seen everywhere. Historically it becomes the theme of evolution; psychologically, the corollary of human nature; educationally, the enemy of learning; socially, the wrong road to change.

Violence, ironically, creates harmony among otherwise warring elements. Left and right agree that the *status quo* breeds violence and merely differ on the cause they attach to it. The rest of us are joined through psychological benefits derived from violence.

We thrill to the threat of violent acts, and we tingle with self-assigned blame for them. Violence, we discover, has the attractiveness of the Devil.

These three paragraphs begin the first chapter of 'an enquiry into the psychology of violence'.[1] I have chosen them because they illustrate vividly both our interest in the problem of violence and many of the reasons for our finding the problem interesting. But violence is a problem for another and quite distinct reason: it is a problem because it is problematic. Despite its pervasive interest, there is surprisingly little agreement on the question of what violence in fact *is*, and what is in fact *violence*.

Rival theories

By far the most significant role in the generation of disputes about violence is played by a consideration which perhaps best accounts for their extreme intractability. This is the fact that definitions of violence have been propounded, and theories of violence advanced, by men who have had very different sorts of *contrast* in mind. Gandhi, with whom modern thinking about the morality of violence begins, contrasted violence with a rather complicated notion of non-violence of which love was an essential ingredient and of which the purpose, inevitably, included a seeking after truth.[2] Gandhi's ideas of non-violence embodied a code for conducting one's life, deviation from which would be likely to involve violence to others. Marxist thinkers have developed a conception of violence which sees society as acting violently towards those of its members whom it exploits or otherwise injures by unjust treatment, or by forcing them to live in degrading conditions and perform alienating tasks for which they are inadequately compensated. The Marxists have in mind a picture of human life as it might be and they see a social order which prevents men from living this life as doing them great violence.[3] Among the many theories of violence that have recently been advanced is one which contrasts violence with an ideal of peace on earth.[4] Included in this definition of violence are those man-made features of the world which would have to be eliminated before the ideal of peace on earth could be said to have been achieved.

Some philosophers have felt that the most important feature of violence is that it involves violation of a person's dignity[5] or of his rights[6] and have adopted conceptions of violence that give these features central place. In contrast to these rather broad conceptions of violence and perhaps as a reaction to them, other philosophers have produced very strict conceptions of violence. Their preoccupation is with law and order, and violence is contrasted with this to yield a narrow definition designed to capture the twin monsters of civil disorder and criminal assault.[7] Other thinkers, impressed by political violence, have further limited the concept of violence by confining its application to acts directed towards political change.[8]

As the problem of violence is seen differently by different thinkers, so this difference in perspective and interest influences the definitions of violence they offer; and the definitions of violence in turn determine the scope of the problem they believe themselves to be facing. The more pervasive and diffuse the problem of violence seems to be, the wider must be the definition which hopes to capture its many aspects. And the wider the definition, the more borderline cases it tends to absorb. Conversely, the more specific the problem seems to be, the narrower and more exclusive is the definition to which it gives rise, thus ruling out many of the cases included in the wider definitions.

It is significant that the champions of various definitions are not even able to agree to differ, but are all evangelists in the cause of their own conception of violence. This disagreement has seemed so intractable and pointless to one philosopher that he has gone so far as to recommend that the word 'violence' be abandoned altogether, as far too confused a notion for consistent use.[9] Although this suggestion provides a possible way out of the difficulty, as there is almost always an alternative form of words that could be used to express the desired points of view, this alternative has proved entirely unattractive. Violence seems to be one of those words that exercise a charm upon people's minds. Its use seems to reveal truths about the world which would be corrupted by a different mode of expression. We might say that these thinkers are seized by a compulsion to describe things in a certain way. But the question remains as to whether this linguistic compulsion is blinding them to the logical objections to what they are doing, or whether perhaps the logical objections are far from clear or decisive.

I have been content merely to indicate the core of the various definitions mentioned and have avoided going at all thoroughly into their content or into their various merits and defects. It is simply the fact of their diversity I wish for the moment to establish and at the same time note the intractability of disputes between rival definitions.

What is violence?

I want now to start by examining afresh the question of what limits can be set to the application of the concept of violence. What can and what can't be called an act of violence? Are some people who use the word violence in the grip of a linguistic compulsion to which clear and decisive objections can be made, or must we perhaps accept a wide and all-embracing definition?

A one-sided diet of analysis and definition has made much moral and political philosophy sterile and unattractive. But here we must dwell briefly on the problem of analysis because if we are to understand the motive for the almost universal 'official' condemnation of violence and also the increasingly obvious radical contempt for what is seen as 'partisan hypocrisy' we first need to know what precisely is being condemned, and why whatever it is is damnable.

Perhaps it would be well to first get clear at least some of the things we would want from any answer to the question: what is violence?

A concept of violence must enable us to distinguish violent methods of dealing with people from methods that are not violent, it must make clear the difference between acts of violence and acts which are not acts of violence. Such a concept will capture what we might call the rape, murder, fire-and-sword paradigm; it will outline a concept which preserves the fearful associations with which we have loaded the notion of violence, it will be such as to include the violent events of history, and finally this concept will show why almost everyone insists on a moral distinction between violent methods and methods which do not involve violence.

The first thing to note is a distinction between violent acts and acts of violence. 'Violent' is an adjective, and a violent act, an act appropriately qualified by that adjective. An act of violence, on the other hand, is an act belonging to a particular category or class of actions not co-extensive with violent acts.

We can state the distinction between violent acts and acts of violence in this way: almost any action a human being can perform can be performed violently. Tom Watson slicing (*per impossibile*) viciously into a bunker, or Mr Gladstone denuding the countryside of trees, are both performing violent acts. Even a cup of tea may be stirred violently. For those who dislike the circularity of saying that a violent act is an act performed violently we can simply say that a violent act is any act appropriately characterised by the following sorts of words taken from the 'violence' entry in *Roget's Thesaurus*: 'inclemency, vehemence, might, impetuosity, boisterousness, turbulence, bluster, uproar, riot, row, rumpus, fury, brute force, outrage, shock, explosion . . .'.[10] The considerations which lead us to classify acts as acts of violence are clearly of a different sort. When trying, for example, to assess the prevalence and the causes of violence in human affairs we are clearly not concerned with a well-hit golf ball; we might say that what concerns us here is what is left when we subtract a violent act from an act of violence. It is important to note that the words 'violent' and 'violence' and the phrases 'act of violence' and 'violent act' are often used indiscriminately between the two senses I have distinguished. In each case, the context must make clear whether the descriptive or classificatory sense of the term is intended.

The descriptive use of 'violent' concentrates on the quality, the character, of the act itself, while it seems that it is the consequences, or perhaps also the intended consequences of such acts, which lead us to classify them as acts of violence. It is natural to regard both these elements, act and consequence or intended consequence, as the severally necessary and jointly sufficient conditions of an act's being an act of violence, and most definitions of violence are built on these elements. Sometimes the violent act, the descriptive element of the definition, is denoted by a phrase like 'extreme physical force' or 'vigorous physical movement' and various different ways have been found of characterising the consequences aimed at. Most usually it is stipulated that the consequences must be harmful, or involve injury or destruction. Some definitions add a further qualification to the effect, that the purposes of the act must be either illegal, immoral or political in nature before they will count as an act of violence. This further qualification is usually invoked to capture what has been called 'the distinctive political concept of violence' and we can ignore it for the moment. For we are at present concerned with what makes an act an act of violence, and we can treat the question of whether such acts must be illegal, immoral or political in character as the icing to be put on or left off the cake when we have the cake before us.

To sum up so far, we have seen that we use the words 'violent' and 'violence' indiscriminately between what can be distinguished as a purely descriptive sense on the one hand, and a classificatory sense on the other. A tentative exploration of the features which lead us to classify an act as an act of violence has yielded a possible definition of an act of violence as a violent act which has or is intended to have harmful, injurious or destructive consequences. Let's now see whether we have, in fact, discovered the facts of violence.

Our definition runs immediately into difficulties, for some acts, while not themselves violent in character, may result in the sort of harm which we would unhesitatingly classify as an act of violence if deliberately inflicted by human agency. For example, if a gangster throws acid in the face of a policeman we would call it an act of violence. If the same gangster were to creep into the same policeman's house at dead of night and gently pour the acid over his face we would, I think, still be inclined to classify it as an act of violence. But perhaps this is because the burning action of acid is itself in a sense violent. A death can, after all, be a violent death even if not brought about by a violent act. A man who is fed a poison which causes him to die writhing and threshing in agony may be said to die a violent death, not because death results from a violent act, but because death itself comes violently. Or, as with Mrs Smallweed's brother in Dickens's *Bleak House* who dies a death that can be attributed to no external cause: 'inborn, inbred, engendered in the corrupted humours of the vicious body itself, and that only — Spontaneous Combustion'.[11] It is hard to imagine a more violent way to die than to be spontaneously consumed in flames.

To turn from fiction to fact, we are told that children in Belfast adopt the following tactic against British soldiers.[12] Here is one of the children describing the method:

That's the street right? These are the lamp-posts and that's the Army Land-Rover coming up the street. You tie your cheese-wire between two of the lamp-posts about six feet up. There's always a soldier standing on the back of the jeep; even with the search lights he can't see the wire in the dark. It's just at the right height to catch his throat.

No violent act but clearly an act of violence. So long as such tactics are employed no one would consider Belfast to be a violence-free city!

These cases seem to indicate that a violent act may not be a necessary condition of an act of violence. In both cases the descriptive element has shifted as it were from the act to the consequences. In the acid case it is the fierce burning action of the acid which provides the descriptive element, and in the case of the children of violence it is the speed of the jeep and the cutting of the wire into the soldier's throat. It might plausibly be argued that in both cases it is the descriptive element which accounts for our readiness to classify them as involving violence. Neither case throws doubt upon the wisdom of an intuitive faith in the fact that there must be something *violent* about acts which we classify as acts of violence. For the future I will refer to all theories incorporating this article of faith, collectively, as 'the strict conception of violence'.

The shift of the descriptive element from the act to the consequences is, however, by no means the end of the trouble for the strict conception of violence.

Non 'violent' violence

Those who accept the strict conception of violence clearly have in mind the rape, murder, fire, and sword paradigm which involves the sudden, forceful, and perhaps unexpected infliction of painful physical injury upon an unwilling victim. Terrorists who machine-gun their victims and bomb their houses are the classic case. But if the terrorists poison the water supply or gas their victims while they sleep, or lock them up in their houses to die of starvation and dehydration, we would not, I think, regard it as mistaken or confused if people continued to speak of 'terrorist violence'! And the terrorists could hardly claim to have renounced violence if they adopted such methods! If it is not inapposite to talk of violence in these cases, the door is open to a wider conception of violence.

If a man is stabbed to death, we do not doubt that he has been the victim of a violent assault. Would we have to alter our judgment if we were later to learn that the stiletto slid between his ribs as gently and as easily as you please? This stiletto point is the thin end of the wedge. For if we are interested in, for example, the question of the prevalence of violence in human affairs, or in comparing the scale of violence in different societies, in different eras, or in assessing the violence of opposing factions, it would be absurd to ignore or exclude methods men find of killing or injuring their fellows which do not happen to involve vigorous direct actions. If, for example, instead of bombs and guns, poison, nerve gas, and exposure to radiation became standard ways of eliminating our fellow men, we would not, I think, be inclined to claim that we had become less violent in our dealings with each other, even though such methods do not involve physical assault or violent actions of any kind.

If we are interested in the question of whether a particular society does or does not use violence as a method of settling differences or resolving disputes, we would certainly not ignore the fact that the society eliminated an opposition group or an unpopular minority by herding them into ghettos where they were left to die of starvation or disease. While such things go on, the claim that mankind is becoming less violent will be viewed with scepticism.

The possible multiplication of such tactics involving no violent act, no physical force on the part of the attacker and causing no violent manner of dying to the victim, is considerable if not infinite. I do not think that we can escape the conclusion that there is something wrong with the strict conception of violence. The examples we have considered should, I think, undermine our faith in the intuition that there has to be something *violent* about violence.

The questions that interest us about violence — questions about its prevalence, its causes, its prevention, questions about when it should be used and why, about whether or not it has been used in particular cases, whether it is on the increase, whether some societies or periods are or were more violent than others — would be trivial questions, if all that they were about was whether or not actions of a particular description were used. Trivial, also, because much of our interest in these questions stems from our concern to solve *the problem of violence*, to minimise its use or even remove it entirely from human affairs, and this we might succeed in doing and yet leave intact all the features of the problem of violence which make a solution desirable. Death, injury and suffering might be just as common as before, only the characteristic complex of actions by which they are inflicted would have changed.

Our interest in all these questions about violence, and in the many cases we want to classify as violence despite the fact that they do not involve any violent acts or cause any violent injuries, surely reflects a concern with the phenomenon of men inflicting injury, suffering or death on one another. We are not so much interested in the particular methods men use to do this, or in the look, the physical appearance of the actions that they use. We are interested in violence because it is a particular kind of activity — the kind of activity in which men inflict injury on one another.

The phenomenon of violence

When we classify an act as an act of violence we are saying that it is part of a single phenomenon, that all men who use violence are involved, in some sense, in the same activity. If we ask what this activity is, the answer that forces itself upon us is, I believe, that it must be the infliction of injury or suffering upon others.

I shall confine the discussion to violence as an activity. This will rule out the violence of hurricanes, earthquakes and other natural phenomena, at least in so far as they are not caused by people negatively. It will also ignore violence caused by men but not attributable to their actions, either because it is accidentally caused, because the men in question do not know what they are doing or lack the requisite mental capacity or otherwise cannot help what they are doing in such a way as to defeat the ascription of an *action* to them. This will leave out of account some events that it will seem proper to call violent but I think that the discussion will gain from being absolved from the responsibility of constantly turning aside and showing how natural calamities and accidental damage or mere behaviour are to be made to 'fit'.

I believe the crucial question is: what is the extent of our violence to one another? This question I think above all others explains and justifies a philosophical approach to the problem of violence and it is this question that I hope this essay will go some way towards answering.

We have so far concluded that the area of activity to which this question, and the other important questions about violence, points, is not the violence of well-hit golf balls or nervously stirred teacups, but what it is that is left when this element has been subtracted from those acts we wish to call acts of violence. We have further concluded that this element is the activity of people inflicting injury or suffering on their fellows.

An act of violence occurs when injury or suffering is inflicted upon a person or persons by an agent who knows (or ought reasonably to have known), that his actions would result in the harm in question.

Let us see how this approach to violence squares with the demands we would make upon any concept of violence which we listed on p. 13. Does it give us a way of distinguishing violent methods from methods that are not violent, and violent acts from acts which are not violent? Clearly it does, for while it may be difficult to tell whether actions are sufficiently forceful or vigorous to count as violence for the purposes of definitions which rely on these elements, and while there may be even greater difficulty in deciding whether the use of force was illegal or immoral for those definitions which include such terms as necessary conditions, human beings have little difficulty in recognising injury and suffering when they see it. For those groups contemplating political or social action the definition will provide a useful way of determining whether or not their proposed actions will commit them to violence, and a commensurately simple way for those whose wish or duty is to oppose such actions, to decide whether or not they are faced with a violent campaign.

The proposed conception of violence does not mention violence to property. I do not think that this form of violence requires a special definition. It seems obvious that damage to or destruction of property or indeed any material object is only significant inasmuch as it is in some way injurious to human beings. And in this context I mean the word 'injury' and its cognates to range over all the senses listed by the *Oxford English Dictionary*. These include: 'Wrongful action or treatment; violation or infringement of another's rights; suffering or mischief wilfully or unjustly inflicted. . . . Hurt or loss caused to or sustained by a person . . . harm, detriment, damage'. These are clearly the most important senses of the word for our purposes but the *OED* also mentions: 'Intentionally hurtful or offensive speech or words; insult, calumny; a taunt, an affront'. While the inclusion of violent speech might seem to trivialise the concept, I do not think this can be ruled out as one of the legitimate senses of violence for two reasons: first because talk about violent language is familiar and natural, but more importantly because speech can cause significant harm and suffering. If the harm of hurtful words is sometimes trivial by comparison, say, with the rape, murder, fire and sword paradigm, so is a feeble punch or glancing blow. This only shows that violence may be more or less serious depending on the injury involved, but this is what one would expect.

Animals have been left out of account. There seems to me to be nothing wrong with viewing violence to animals in a similar way to viewing violence to persons, but our interest will be solely with persons.[13]

The second requirement of a definition of violence was that it capture the rape, murder, fire and sword paradigm and preserve the fearful associations with which the notion of violence has been loaded. How does our concept of violence

fare in this respect? The rape, murder, fire and sword paradigm will clearly remain a central case, for it is not only a
paradigm of violence but it is also, of course, a paradigm of
the infliction of injury and suffering. Nor is there any reason
why violence as we have defined it should lose any of its
fearful associations. Our concept embraces all the cases
falling within the strict conception of violence but adds a
further range of cases which, like those of the strict conception, range from the truly fearful to the trivial.

Finally, does our definition of violence preserve the
intelligibility of a moral preference for actions which do not
involve violence over those which do? The answer to this
question must be 'yes', for without knowing more about
individual cases it must be morally preferable to choose ways
of acting that do not involve injury and suffering to others
over those which do, other things, of course, being equal.

The violence of normal times

The violent events of history, the wars and revolutions, will
clearly conform to our conception, but more importantly
another class of events noted as violence by far fewer histori-
ans than are the strict cases, will also fall within our purview.
I am thinking of the sort of conditions to which so many
revolutions were a response, the sort of conditions which
Barrington Moore Jr called 'the violence of normal times'.[14]
For Barrington Moore Jr 'to dwell on the horrors of revolutionary violence while forgetting that of "normal" times, is
merely partisan hypocrisy'.[15] The violence of normal times is
perhaps a controversial notion. The justification of such a
position, however, depends upon our being able to show how
starvation, disease, industrial injury and much else are among
the things we do to one another. This we will begin to do in
the next chapter. For the moment, and anticipating success,
if the case for 'quiet' violence can be made out it will be
important to have a conception of violence that can accommodate the violence of normal times.

We have moved very rapidly to a radical conception of
violence and it may seem that in jumping so quickly from the

obvious inadequacies of the strict conception of violence to this rather broad conception, we must inevitably have passed over a number of distinctions that might have enabled us to keep the strictness of the strict view and thus hold on to our intuition that there has to be something *violent* about violence. I do not think that we have passed over any distinctions that would enable us to escape the conclusions we have reached. For if we are interested in the question of the extent of our violence to one another, I do not see how we can fail to consider injury or suffering inflicted on a person by an agent who knows, or ought reasonably to have known, that his actions would result in such harm. Any treatment of the phenomenon of human violence which left such actions out of account would be perversely narrow.

It will be important not only to have such a wide conception of violence but to emphasise the consequences of having one. The full weight of moral disapproval rightly falls on those who employ violence; the problem is that moral disapproval falls, as it is wont to fall, highly selectively. James Callaghan, then Home Secretary, said *à propos* a student demonstration[16]

> I am worried about the freedom which is invaded by those who believe they can secure by violence what they cannot get by reason. . . . These are violations of freedom in my view — the freedom of the majority, whether their views are accepted or not, and I must be on my guard to repel that invasion of freedom.

Sir Harold Wilson, when Prime Minister, commenting on a terrorist bombing, said 'the use of violence whatever the motive may be, if there is a motive, must be treated as a major crime.'[17] More recently Sir Robert Mark, former Metropolitan Police Commissioner, said that after forty years in the police he had come to the conclusion that 'the worst crime of all is the use of violence in pursuit of political or industrial ends . . . because that threatens freedom itself . . . and I think the second cause for very great concern is the acceptance by people generally of violence used in that way.'[18]

Statements such as these by eminent men commonly and rightly command general agreement, but they tend to be taken selectively in two ways. First, it is often assumed that the danger of violence comes exclusively from its use by mobs, workers, students and other unruly citizenry, whereas George Rudé and others have reminded us it is very often the authorities who are perpetrators of the greater violence. Rudé, for example, calculates that between 1736 and 1848 crowds caused the death of not more than a dozen people while the response of the authorities was to hang 118 people while a further 630 were shot dead by troops.[19]

The second way in which violence is condemned selectively is that the violence of normal times emphasised by Barrington Moore Jr is not equally condemned, it is not even equally recognised! Nor, more importantly, do people try equally hard to eradicate it. This leads to an overwhelming sense of bad faith where 'Thesaurian violence' is unequivocably damned and the very people who are loudest in its condemnation are themselves very often responsible for the much more serious harm which comes about as a result of omissions or non-violent action.

It is to an examination of precisely how such harm comes about that we must now turn.

Chapter 3

Negative actions

Examples

The idea that if we are able to change things, to elect not to do so is also to determine what will happen in the world, is very old indeed. For obvious reasons, the idea is only employed when the things that happen are of some significance. The importance of the idea and its history stem from those cases where harm occurs which might have been averted or in which harm will occur unless it is averted. In such cases, many men found it natural not only to blame those who could have prevented the harm yet did not do so, but also to think of such men as having brought the harm about, as being its cause.

I do not know when this idea first occurred. Plutarch makes use of it, as does Jesus,[1] John Bromyard, a fourteenth-century Chancellor of Cambridge, gives it most eloquent expression, and it is, of course, one of the main themes of Shakespeare's *Measure for Measure*. In modern times it has been associated most strongly with Marx, Engels, and Marxist thinkers. In their hands it has been used as a weapon in the controversy about 'violence'. Marxists have argued that deaths caused by the indifference and neglect of society or its rulers must be seen as being as much a part of human violence as the violent acts of revolutionaries.

The idea that where men are able to prevent the occurrence of harm to their fellows but fail to do so, they may be responsible for the consequent injury, is probably as old as any thinking about responsibility. Plutarch, for example, makes the point that a man who fails to protect another from a death he was able to prevent is just as guilty of that man's death as if he had wielded the sword himself. Talking of the revenge of the Triumvirs in his life of Mark Antony, Plutarch states: 'At the end of all this bartering of one death for another, they [the Triumvirs] were just as guilty of the deaths of those whom they abandoned as of those whom they seized.'[2]

In his guide for preachers, John Bromyard[3] imagines the Last Judgment:[4]

On the left, before the supreme Judge's throne stand 'the harsh lords, who plundered the people of God with grievous fines, amercements and exactions, . . . the wicked ecclesiastics, who failed to nourish the poor with the goods of Christ . . . as they should have done. . . . Then the oppressed bring a fearful indictment against their oppressors. . . . 'We hungered and thirsted and were afflicted with cold and nakedness. And those robbers yonder gave not our own goods to us when we were in want, neither did they feed and clothe us out of them. But their hounds and horses and apes, the rich, the powerful, the abounding, the gluttons, the drunkards and their prostitutes they fed and clothed with them, and allowed us to languish in want. . . . 'O just God, mighty judge, the game was not fairly divided between them and us. Their satiety was our famine; their merriment was our wretchedness; their jousts and tournaments were our torments. . . . Their feasts, delectations, pomps, vanities, excesses and superfluities were our fastings, penalties, wants, calamities and spoliation. The love-ditties and laughter of their dances were our mockery, our groanings and remonstrations. They used to sing . . . "well enough! well enough!" . . . and we groaned, saying . . . "Woe to us! Woe to us!" '

The most compelling and coherent statement of this view occurs in Engels's book *The Condition of the Working Class in England*.[5] It is worth quoting at some length:[6]

If one individual inflicts a bodily injury upon another which leads to the death of the person attacked we call it manslaughter; on the other hand, if the attacker knows beforehand that the blow will be fatal we call it murder. Murder has also been committed if society places hundreds of workers in such a position that they inevitably come to premature and unnatural ends. Their death is as violent as if they had been stabbed or shot. Murder has been committed if thousands of workers have been deprived of the necessities of life or if they have been forced into a situation in which it is impossible for them to survive. Murder has been committed if the workers have been forced by the strong arm of the law to go on living under such conditions until death inevitably releases them. Murder has been committed if society knows perfectly well that thousands of workers cannot avoid being sacrificed so long as these conditions are allowed to continue. Murder of this sort is just as culpable as the murder committed by an individual. But if society murders a worker it is a treacherous stab in the back against which a worker cannot defend himself. At first sight it does not appear to be murder at all because responsibility for the death of the victim cannot be pinned on any individual assailant. Everyone is responsible and yet no one is responsible, because it appears as if the victim has died from natural causes. If a worker dies no one places the responsibility for his death on society, though some would realise that society has failed to take steps to prevent the victim from dying. But it is murder all the same.

Christopher Caudwell,[7] writing in 1938, makes use of a similar analysis of social relations:[8]

> Thus, just as much as in slave-owning society, bourgeois society turns out to be a society built on violent coercion of men by men, the more violent in that while the master must feed and protect his slave, whether he works or not, the bourgeois employer owes no obligation to the free labourer.

Caudwell concludes, in agreement with Engels, that the absence of an individual assailant cannot affect responsibility:[9]

> The fact that one participates passively in bourgeois economy that one does not oneself wield the bludgeon or fire the cannon, as far from being a defence really makes one's position more disgusting. . . .

Ten years later Harold Orlans[10] summed up his experience of conditions in an American mental hospital, in which he had

worked as a conscientious objector during the Second World
War, as follows:[11]

> It is in the murder by neglect of decrepit old men that I
> believe the closest analogy is to be found with death camp
> murders. The asylum murders are passive; the Auschwitz
> murders active . . . but otherwise their logic is the same.

Barrington Moore, Jr warned that the death toll of the
French revolutionary Terror must be seen as a response to
'the prevailing social order', which 'always grinds out its
toll of unnecessary death year after year'.[12] 'It would be
enlightening', Moore continues, 'to calculate the death rate
of the *ancien régime* from such factors as preventable starvation and injustice'. Moore's point is that 'to dwell on the
horrors of revolutionary violence while forgetting that of
"normal" times is merely partisan hypocrisy.'[13]

Marx himself gives repeated examples of the injury, shame,
degradation, and death suffered every day by the working
class and directly caused by the capitalist economy. In the
chapter entitled 'Machinery and Modern Industry' in volume
1 of *Capital*[14] he spends most of his time pointing out the
'antagonistic and murderous side' of modern manufacture.
'One of the most shameful, the most dirty, and the worst
paid kinds of labour' is that of the rag-sorters who 'are the
medium for the spread of small-pox and other infectious
diseases and are themselves the first victims'. We learn that
'it is impossible for a child to pass through the purgatory of
a tile field without great moral degradation'. . . . We are
shown how the increase in the incidence of consumption
among lace-makers rose from 1 in 45 in 1852 to 1 in 8 in
1860, and that 'fearful increase in death from starvation
during the last ten years in London runs parallel with the
extension of machine-sewing'. 'In one scutching mill at
Kildinan, near Cork,' we are told, 'there occurred between
1852 and 1856, six fatal accidents and sixty mutilations;
every one of which might have been prevented by the simplest appliances, at the cost of a few shillings. These mutilations are of the most fearful nature. In many cases a quarter
of the body is torn from the trunk, and either involves death,
or a future of wretched incapacity and suffering.' Marx's
emphasis is on the harm caused to human beings by their

being forced to work in injurious conditions and by the failure of the employers or society generally to prevent suffering and death which could easily and at little cost be prevented. Whenever harm comes to workers in any way connected with their employment or the conditions of their lives which their work or lack of work forces upon them, the employers and society at large treat the harm as a natural calamity about which it is impossible to do anything. Marx believes that where human intervention could prevent this harm, then failure to prevent the harm must be seen as a cause:[15]

> Wherever there is a working day without restriction as to length, wherever there is night work and unrestricted waste of human life, there the slightest obstacle presented by the nature of the work to a change for the better is soon looked upon as an everlasting barrier erected by Nature. No poison kills vermin with more certainty than the Factory Act removes such everlasting barriers. No one made a greater outcry over 'impossibilities' than our friends the earthenware manufacturers. In 1864 however, they were brought under the act, and within sixteen months every 'impossibility' had vanished.

Finally, I should like to cite the brief statement of an anonymous witness to a contemporary tragedy. Michael Elkins, broadcasting from Jerusalem for BBC Radio News, reported that an eyewitness to the suicide squad massacre at Jerusalem airport which the Arab terrorists achieved by smuggling guns and bombs aboard an Israeli airliner, said: 'Don't tell me anyone searched the suitcases of those men — whoever let those men on the plane is also guilty of murder.'

All of these views emphasise both that the 'normal' conditions of society are vicious and injurious and that responsibility rests as much with those who *allow such states of affairs to continue*, as with those who *brought them about*. It will be obvious that all these examples depend at some point on recognition of the causal efficacy of omissions: workers are murdered because conditions in which they cannot survive are 'allowed to continue', one 'participates passively' in violent coercion, decrepit old men are murdered 'by neglect', the *ancien régime* has a high death rate because of 'preventable starvation and injustice', death and mutilation 'might have been prevented by the simplest appliances at the cost of a few shillings'.

It is a commonplace that negative events or static conditions can be causes. As Hart and Honoré[16] emphasise, 'there is no convenient substitute for statements that the lack of rain was the cause of the failure of a corn crop, the icy condition of the road was the cause of the accident, the failure of the signalman to pull the lever was the cause of the train smash'.[17] Where, as in the case of the signalman, a man's omission to do something which would have prevented an occurrence makes him the cause of that occurrence, it is natural to think of the omission as something that the man does. I will, therefore, following Bentham,[18] call such omissions 'negative actions'.[19]

Bentham distinguished between positive and negative actions very simply; 'to strike' he said, 'is a positive act; not to strike on a certain occasion a negative one' but Bentham failed to give any account of how to distinguish the occasions on which not to strike is a negative act from those on which it isn't. The crucial question is how are we to distinguish those occasions on which a man's failure to do something which would have prevented or checked an occurrence, makes him its cause, from those on which it doesn't. If my aged parent lives with me, bedridden and helpless, then if I discontinue my daily visits to feed and care for him he will die and my neglect will be the cause. But if I do not cut his throat, my failure to kill him will not be cited as the cause of his living to a ripe old age.

An adequate account of this distinction and consequently an adequate account of negative actions is crucial because much of the injury and suffering to human beings in the world is preventable. How much of this suffering is attributable to our failure to prevent it? How much of this suffering must be seen as part of our violence to one another? This latter is a question to which we have already given an answer in Chapter 2.

If it is true that we are causally responsible for the harm we might have prevented, then the argument of the previous chapter shows why such harm must be seen as part of our violence to one another. We must now try to provide an adequate account of negative actions and so see whether the view that men are causally responsible for the harm they could have prevented, can be sustained.

D'Arcy and expectation

Since Bentham's time, several attempts have been made to give an adequate account of when a failure to act has consequences, and when it does not. In what follows, I shall consider three of the most influential of such attempts and argue that their deficiences point the way to a more satisfactory account of negative actions, an account, moreover, which is clearly the one upon which the conception of violence developed in Chapter 1 relies.

The crucial question is: in what circumstances is it appropriate to say that Y is a consequence of not doing X? Eric D'Arcy asks this question, and answers[20] that Y is called a consequence of A's not doing X only when:

1   doing X is a standard way of preventing Y.
2   A is in some way expected to do X.
3   X is required of A in order that something such as Y should not happen.

D'Arcy makes it clear that A may be expected to do X, in the requisite sense of 'expected', if either, (a) ' "X" is something that A usually does, or people usually do, in the situation in question', or (b) ' "X" is required of him by some rule with which he is expected to comply'. 'This may of course be some moral rule, or principle; but it will often be a non-moral rule.' The rule which requires X of A will often be, on D'Arcy's account, a catch-all Benthamite duty of beneficence which will cover 'things which we should, or ought to do or not do to others, even when they are not required by virtue of office, voluntary undertaking, or special relationship'.

D'Arcy explains his set of conditions under which Y will be a consequence of A's not doing X, as follows:[21]

A can . . . be held responsible for Y only to the extent that some relationship of cause and consequence exists between them; the only such relationship is that which exists by virtue of the connection of each with X; and, by hypothesis, X connects them only to this extent, that X is enjoined upon A in order that something such as Y should not happen.

And he concludes that:[22]

in moral investigations, at least, the charge that A did not do X with the result that Y happened will . . . be successfully rebutted if it can be shown, not only that doing X was something which was not required of A: but even that it was not required of him in order that things such as Y might not happen.

On D'Arcy's view, before we can say that A's failure to do X caused any result whatsoever, it must *already* be the case that X is expected or required of A. For if A is not already connected with X by some duty, then when X is not performed with the consequence that Y happens, A will not be connected to X, and therefore not to Y either.

D'Arcy has put his model together back-to-front, for his condition that 'X is required of A in order that something such as Y should not happen' would be pointless if it did not exploit our understanding of the causal connection between the failure of X and the occurrence of Y. D'Arcy's own explication of the notion of beneficence confirms this. Beneficence, it will be remembered, covers 'things which we should, or ought to do or not do to others'. One of D'Arcy's examples (derived from Bentham) of the exercise of this duty is the following: 'If a drunkard falls face downwards into a puddle, and is in danger of drowning, a bystander has a duty at least to lift his head a little to one side and so save him'. . . . But our duty is not to go around lifting the heads of drunks, *and so save them*, our duty *is* to save them if we can. And we have this duty, because to fail to save someone we could save would be the death of him. It would not be the death of him because we have the duty, it would be the death of him because we fail to save him. His death is a consequence of our failure, whether we have a duty to save him or not (we might have a duty to kill this particular man and discharge it by failing to save him). It is not the existence of the duty that makes the death of the drunk a consequence of our failure to save him, rather it is the fact that unless we save him he will die that makes it our duty to save him.

If ever the duty of beneficence was owed, it was owed surely to the man who fell among thieves on the Jericho road. The thieves left him half dead, and he would perhaps have perished had the Samaritan followed the priest and the Levite and left him untended. The probable consequence of passing by on the other side would be the death of the man. To see this is to see a causal connection between the failure to tend the man and his death. And it is because we understand this connection that we see the point of the parable, that we realise why it is that the priest and the Levite ought to have tended the man. We do not need to postulate a duty of beneficence to explain how the neglect of the passers-by might well have resulted in the man's death, rather we need to understand the causal connection between *neglect* and *death* to see why anyone might be required to tend him.

Casey and role playing

John Casey, in a recent discussion on this problem,[23] notes that 'the introduction of a statement which claims to give the *cause* of some event presupposes a pattern of normal expectations such that what will count as the cause of the event is, as it were, an intrusion into the pattern of expectations.' Casey goes on to state the conditions under which failure to act can have causal status in terms similar to D'Arcy's. 'If a man does not do X, we cannot properly say that his not doing X is the cause of some result Y unless, in the normal course of events, he could have been expected to do X.' Casey then argues that a man can be held 'personally responsible' for something (and Casey means by this term of art roughly what Hart means by his term 'liability responsibility', namely, that the person is responsible in some way for which he may appropriately be praised or blamed) if (and only if):[24]

(a) his actions (or omissions) are causally responsible for it;

(b) the outcome has some importance in terms of what he might be expected to do; in general that is, in terms of a pattern of role responsibilities, in the context of which he acts;

(c) normal conditions exist (i.e. no excusing conditions).
Casey notes that 'the correctness of saying that condition (a)
is satisfied rests on a rule of conversational propriety which is
equivalent to the assertion of condition (b).' This note is
necessary because, if 'the introduction of a statement which
claims to give the *cause* of some event presupposes a pattern
of normal expectations such that what will count as the cause
of the event is . . . an intrusion into the pattern of expectations', we must have some idea of what our normal expectations are. And if a failure to act is to be identified and given
causal status, the normal conditions in the light of which it is
a *failure* to act must be known. In knowing what a man is
expected to do, we know the normal conditions; when a man
fails to do what is expected of him, we can see that the failure is an intrusion into the pattern of normal expectations,
and we are then able to say that certain events are the *results*
of his failure. Furthermore, Casey believes that what he calls
'a man's role' defines what sort of agent he is, and what are
his responsibilities and obligations, *prior* to any particular
case.

This is, of course, sometimes true. The cultivation of his
own garden is, if he does not employ a gardener, part of a
man's 'role responsibilities' in the broad sense in which Casey
uses the term. If the garden grows to seed and becomes
possessed by things rank and gross in nature, the owner is
responsible; we know this prior to the deterioration of the
garden, because we know who is responsible for its upkeep.
But sometimes we know what a man's responsibilities and
obligations are only *because* we see that failure to act in a
certain way will result in the occurrence of the sort of things
that matter to us all. And where this is so, Casey's notion of
a man's role will fail to provide a way of specifying what a
man's obligations are which is independent of the consequences of his not fulfilling them. If, sometimes, X is only
expected of someone because we see that Y will happen if he
does not do X, then we cannot use the fact that X is expected of that person to prove that Y is a result of his not doing
X. In these cases it is not the fact that X is expected of a man
that allows us to say that his not doing X makes him causally
responsible for Y, but rather the fact that we see him to be

causally responsible for Y shows us that X was expected or required of him. It is as if we had spent some time and trouble establishing that eggs are a necessary condition for the existence of chickens, and some ungrateful person innocently asked about the origin of eggs.

But Casey uses his concept of 'role' not only to amplify the notion of what is expected of a man, but also to argue that a man's own interpretation of the part he has assigned himself in the drama can limit his responsibility for consequences. Indeed, he sometimes seems to be saying that if a man defines his role sufficiently narrowly there may even be *no* consequences of his adopting such a role.

Casey considers the dilemma of the obstetrician who is faced with a woman in labour who will die unless a craniotomy operation is performed to extract the foetus from the womb by crushing its skull. The alternative to a craniotomy, which will kill the foetus, is to let the woman die and deliver the baby alive by *post mortem* Caesarian section.

From the obstetrical case in which either the mother or the foetus may be saved, but not both, Casey argues that to say that in refusing to kill the foetus a doctor lets the mother die, presupposes a certain view of the medical role. On a conservative view of the medical role it might, according to Casey reasonably be thought that a doctor's job was to 'assist' certain natural processes and procure health only by certain means.

On this view, if a doctor killed a healthy foetus in order to procure the health of the mother, 'he would not be simply curing a disorder of the mother's body . . . but doing something else. He might be deciding which of two lives was more valuable, or who had the better right to life. Whatever the merits of his decision that would be outside his role as an obstetrician.'[25] And so, Casey continues, 'if killing the child is *ruled out* by the medical role, then this will prohibit our taking (the doctor's) killing the child as something we could reasonably expect. Hence the correctness of our ascribing causal responsibility in the present case will depend upon the acceptability of some particular conception of the doctor's role.'[26]

If we conceive of our role as good citizens as involving

unquestioning obedience to the commands of government, we do not escape responsibility for what we do or fail to do in response to those commands, even though disobedience is ruled out by our conception of the citizen's role. Acceptance of this role does not prevent our being responsible for its consequences any more than it prevents there being consequences. Casey seems to see this, for he says later on in the paper:[27]

What I have called a man's 'role' defines the sort of agent
he is and what are his responsibilities and obligations,
prior to any particular case. To suggest that a man must
accept responsibility for all the foreseen consequences of
what he does or refrains from doing is really to refuse to
accept the notion of a 'role' in this sense at all.

and Casey concludes:[28]

A man may believe that one should always aim at being a
certain sort of man, whatever the consequence. One
should always be a man of honour, or *kalos kai agathos*,
or magnanimous, not just as a means to an end, but
because that is the right sort of man to be . . . . Any
argument for or against his stance would have to be
persuasive; it would involve the weighing up and
appreciation of one sort of character, of one sort of life
as against another.

Casey seems to have moved from the view that 'the correctness of ascribing causal responsibility . . . will depend upon some particular conception of the doctor's role', that is, from the view that if the conservative doctor refuses to kill the foetus, whatever then happens to the mother cannot be a consequence of the refusal; to the view that although it is a consequence of the refusal, the doctor cannot be held accountable unless we accept a different, consequentialist view of the doctor's role. We may agree with Casey that a man may believe that it is right to be a certain sort of man whatever the consequences and that any argument against his stance would have to be persuasive, but that by no means rules out the possibility of that man's being both causally responsible and accountable for the consequences of preserving his integrity as a certain sort of man. The man might accept that the price he pays for the preservation of his honour in terms of adverse consequences to others is high. He might indeed make a point of recognising the tragic necessity of accepting full responsibility for the harmful consequences which that conception of his honour would not let him prevent.

Casey is trying to make his notion of 'role' do more work than it can bear. His argument requires that if a course of action is ruled out by a particular conception of a man's role, he can only be held responsible for the 'consequences' of failing to pursue that course of action by those who do not accept that conception of his role.

Let us suppose that a hospital orderly's job is just to clean up the wards and act as a porter, and let us further suppose that he has been expressly forbidden to interfere with the patients at all or with their treatment. The orderly accepts his role and recognises the wisdom of his regarding the treatment of patients as quite beyond his duties. One day, when for some reason none of the medical staff are about, a patient begins to haemorrhage. The orderly realises that if the blood flow is not staunched the patient will surely die, and moreover, the orderly himself knows how to bind the wound. If the orderly does nothing and lets the patient die, he is causally responsible for the patient's death despite the fact that his role precludes interference. And this is so, even if we all feel that this particular patient (a particularly vicious dictator) ought to be killed. It is failure to save someone who *can* be saved that carries with it causal responsibility, not failure to save someone who *ought* to be saved.

Barrington Moore Jr[29] as we have seen, warned that the death toll of the French revolutionary Terror must be seen as a response to 'the prevailing social order' which 'always grinds out its toll of unnecessary death year after year'. 'It would be enlightening', Barrington Moore Jr continues, 'to calculate the death rate of the *ancien régime* from such factors as preventable starvation and injustice.' Clearly, the functionaries and the privileged of the *ancien régime* did not see the deaths of the peasants and workers as any of their business, as in any way connected with their own lives. This was probably true not only where the deaths were caused by neglect but also where they were caused by positive actions. When the Marquis de St Evrémonde rides down and kills a child with his carriage, he is more concerned that the dead child may have injured his horses than he is with the fact that he has killed another human being. He throws out a gold coin and drives away, 'with the air of a man who had accidently broken some common thing, and had paid for it, and could afford to pay for it'.[30]

Even the Marquis de St Evrémonde recognises that he has broken something. He differs from us in his assessment of how much that matters and consequently over the need to drive more carefully or take avoiding action. He would probably accept that his failure to take avoiding action or issue the appropriate instructions to his coachman was the cause of the 'breakage'.

Someone who fails to see that his failure to prevent preventable suffering becomes in turn a cause of such suffering has contracted a sort of blindness akin to what Wittgenstein called 'aspect blindness'.[31] It is the failure to see what is there to be seen; it is the failure to see a connection that exists. The man whose role makes him myopic to consequences is not merely a man with one set of ideals rather than another, whom we can, at best, *persuade* to change his values; he is a man who is blind to certain things. One cannot persuade the myopic to see, but one can improve the lighting and provide spectacles.

The point is not that one has to be a consequentialist, but that the adoption of certain roles, certain sets of values and ideals, does have certain consequences. The consequences are the price that is paid for the maintenance of high ideals. Maybe the ideals are worth it; maybe they are not. That is another question, and one to which we will return.[32]

Hart, Honoré, and normalcy

In their book, *Causation in the Law*,[33] H.L.A. Hart and A.M. Honoré deal extensively with the question of the causal status of omissions. Their account relies heavily on some idea of normalcy. 'When things go wrong and we then ask for the cause, we ask this on the assumption that the environment persists unchanged, and something has "made the difference" between what normally happens in it and what has happened on this occasion.'[34] On their account, when an omission has causal status, it has that status because it constitutes a departure from what normally happens:[35]

> What is taken as normal for the purpose of the distinction
> between cause and mere conditions is very often an
> artefact of human habit, custom or convention. This is so
> because men have discovered that nature is not only
> sometimes harmful *if* we intervene, but is also
> sometimes harmful *unless* we intervene, and have
> developed customary techniques, procedures and routines
> to counteract such harm. These have become a second
> 'nature' and so a second 'norm'. The effect of drought is
> regularly neutralized by government precautions in
> preserving water or food; disease is neutralized by
> inoculation; rain by the use of umbrellas. When such
> man-made normal conditions are established deviation
> from them will be regarded as exceptional and so rank
> as the cause of harm.

Hart and Honoré emphasise that deviation from customary techniques will rank as a cause, not because harm always results from such deviation but because the 'omitted precaution would have arrested the harm'. This is certainly so, and it is an important point, but must the techniques have become customary, the procedures and routines *normal*, the method of prevention *standard*, before we can say that their omission caused some outcome?

At what point does the failure to neutralise the harmful effects of disease come to rank as the cause of those harmful effects? On the Hart-Honoré view this happens only when the practice of inoculation has become 'a second "nature" and so a second "norm" '. Let us suppose that a vaccine against cancer is developed, tried, and tested at a university or by a drug manufacturer, that its discovery is made known by the firm which developed it, but that no one takes steps to make it generally available or to provide money for its mass production. Are we not entitled, indeed required, to conclude that a government, for example, or a drug company, which continues to allow people to die of cancer, when they could so easily be saved, is responsible for their deaths, indeed, that it has killed them? And are we not entitled to say this even though no customary practice of vaccination against cancer has become second nature to the society in question? Hart and Honoré might reply that while vaccination against cancer has not become customary, the practice of inoculation is a standard method of prevention of disease, and that it is this practice which makes it possible to say that the failure to make available any new vaccine may involve causal responsibility for the continuing prevalence of the disease.

But we can push our enquiry further back and ask whether, when it had become clear that Jenner's vaccine was successful in preventing smallpox, it would have been necessary to wait until the practice of inoculation had become standard *before* it would be correct to cite failure to vaccinate as a cause, perhaps the most significant cause, of an epidemic.[36]

When in 1939 Howard Florey and Ernst Chain and their team concentrated and purified Fleming's antibiotic penicillin and demonstrated its curative properties, it would surely have been ludicrous to suggest that it was necessary to wait until its use had become standard before anyone was in a position to realise that any failure to put it into mass production would cost thousands of lives. Indeed, its use could not become standard until it was put into mass production, and there would be no reason to put it into mass production, and thus make its use standard, if it were not already obvious that to fail to do so would cost lives.[37]

When is it appropriate to say that Y is a consequence of A's not doing X? The idea that a prerequisite of our saying that A's failure to do X caused Y is that X be somehow expected of A, which is employed by Hart and Honoré, D'Arcy and Casey, is probably correct for the majority of negative actions. The fact that someone normally does X, or that it is expected for some other reason that someone will do X, makes the non-occurrence of X on a particular occasion something that calls for explanation. Or again, if A is required to do X, we have a reason for wanting to know if X has happened and, if it has not happened, for wondering why not. In either case, we first expect X of A, and whatever reason we have for so doing also shows why the non-occurrence of X calls for an explanation at all, and indicates the direction in which to look for an answer. If we know it is the porter's job to raise the college flag at daybreak and at noon the college flagstaff is naked, we may want to know why the flag has not been raised, and the somnolence of the porter satisfies our curiosity. But the nakedness of flagpoles is unproblematic unless, *because* we know the porter's duties, we have some reason for expecting to see them clothed with flags. Where harm to human beings is concerned, however, our interest needs no special occasion. We are always interested in the causes of harm to ourselves and our fellows.

The discussion of the theories of Hart and Honoré, D'Arcy and Casey seems to indicate that the moment we realise that harm to human beings could be prevented, we are entitled to see the failure to prevent it as a cause of harm. As it stands, this statement seems too comprehensive in scope. We do not usually think of the man who fails to give money to save the victims of famine abroad as a killer, even though we know that even a small donation would save lives. Still less, perhaps, do we think of society as guilty of massive carnage because it continues to allow the use of motor vehicles, although we know that were motor vehicles to be banned or, less drastically, their permitted speed severely limited, thousands of lives would be saved each year. That we do not usually speak of causes in these cases seems to show that there is something wrong with saying that the moment we realise that harm could be avoided, we are entitled to see the failure to prevent it as a cause of the harm. What appears to be wrong with the statement, and certainly the criticism that Hart and Honoré would level at it, is that it involves a confusion between causes and mere conditions. Wherever there is a possibility of preventing harm, its non-prevention is a necessary condition of the harm's occurring. But is something more required for a necessary condition to become a cause?

Hart and Honoré give a detailed account of just what more this is. They distinguish 'mere conditions' from 'causes' properly so called.[38] Mere conditions are 'just those (factors) which are present alike both in the case where such accidents occur and in the cases where they do not, and it is this consideration that leads us to reject them as the cause of the accident, even though it is true that without them the accident would not have occurred'. It is plain, of course, that to cite factors which are present both in the case of disaster and of normal functioning would explain nothing; such factors do not 'make the difference' between disaster and normal function. Hart and Honoré emphasise that what is or is not normal functioning can be relative to the context of any given enquiry in two ways: either because some feature which pervades most contexts has been specifically excluded in a particular case, or because 'in one and the same case . . . the distinction between cause and condition can be drawn in different ways. The cause of a great famine in India may be identified by the Indian peasant as the drought, but the World Food Authority may identify the Indian government's failure to build up reserves as the cause and the drought as a mere condition.'[39] Hart and Honoré suppose that what we want to know, when we ask for a causal explanation in cases like this, is what made *these* people die of starvation when normally *they* would have lived? And the answer given is that one can say that what made this difference was the Indian government's failure to build up reserves – 'an abnormal failure of a normal condition'.

But what if normal functioning is always a disaster? Every year, just like clockwork, the poor and the jobless, the aged and the infirm, suffer terribly, and many of them die. What is the cause? The myopic view is that they die because they are poor and jobless, aged and infirm. That is what distinguishes them from those who do not suffer, from those who do not die. But the World Moral Authority may identify the neglect of other members of society or of the government as the cause, and the other features as mere conditions. And surely the World Moral Authority's causal explanation is not upset by the discovery that this society normally neglects its weakest members, that there is no difference between what they did this year and what they always do, that caring for their needy is by no means an established procedure with them.

Of course, Hart and Honoré can retreat to a second line of defence which their account affords. They can say that, while this society may be callous, provision for the needy is none the less a well-established procedure among humane people, and it is this that allows us to cite neglect as the cause of suffering in the case; or in the case of the Indian famine, that building up of reserves is a technique for preventing famine established at least since the time of Moses. This can only be a temporary line of defence, because there was a time when these precautions against harm were not the normal practice, and at that time, when men were wondering what was the cause of all the misery they saw about them, they did not ask themselves: 'Why are these people suffering when *normally* they would not suffer?' But 'Why are these people suffering *when they could have been spared* their suffering?'

When we are seeking a causal explanation of the disasters that overtake human beings, we are often not seeking to explain why a disaster occurred on this occasion when normally it would not have occurred, but why it occurred on this occasion when it need not have done. Human life is often such a chapter of disasters that what we want explained is why these disasters happen when they could have been prevented. In these cases the question that interests us and the question that must interest anyone who wishes to explain why human beings so often needlessly come to grief, is not: *what made the difference*, but, *what might have made the difference*? In the case of the Indian famine the 'mere' conditions will be the drought, the failure of the crops, and so on, the cause will be the failure of the Indian government to build up reserves or perhaps the failure of other governments to send speedy and sufficient aid. When we are looking for what might make the difference between harm's occurring and its not occurring, anything that could have been done to prevent the harm in question is a likely candidate for causal status.

Negative causation and negative actions

So far, we have been interested in the question of when a failure to act has consequences and when it does not, in when Y is a consequence of A's failure to do X and when it is not. Our interest has been quite undiscriminating between the circumstances in which it is correct to say that Y is a *consequence* of A's actions or omissions and those in which one can say that A *caused* Y or that A is *responsible* for Y. But when we say that someone was the cause of harm to human beings, we are singling him out as the author of the harm (or at least as *one of* the authors), we are saying that he is responsible for it and probably that he is to blame (or if, for some reason, we feel that the harm was well-deserved, those responsible might be praised). Praise or blame is usually appropriate where harm to human beings is knowingly caused. If we think that a particular method of preventing a particular harm is for not using it, and it is the only way that the harm could have been averted, we are unlikely to cite the failure to use the method as a *cause* of the harm, even though the fact that the harm occurred is, of course, a *consequence* of the failure.

But what do these facts about the words we usually choose in different situations indicate about negative causation? If we think that a possible method of preventing harm is ineligible, that its use is for some reason completely out of the question, then we are unlikely to see it as something that might have made the difference (or that made the difference) between the harm's occurring and its not occurring. We just do not think of it as something that 'could have been done' to avert the disaster.

People are likely to differ crucially about just how viable options of saving others are. Suffering people are likely to see the possibility of their sufferings being relieved as highly eligible, but those who would have to make sacrifices to bring relief are likely to think differently, especially if they have interests which would be permanently prejudiced by any change in the *status quo*.

Of course, if someone claims out of the blue that failure to do something hitherto judged to be quite out of the question amounts to murder, then some explanation at least is owed. But the legitimacy of claiming that a failure to exercise a particular option is causing death does not depend on our agreeing that the option should be or should have been exercised.[40]

I have suggested that where Y involves harm to human beings, then Y will be a consequence of A's not doing X simply where X would have prevented Y and A could have done X. Where the doing of X is considered to be out of the question, we tend to act and talk as though the condition that A could have done X is not satisfied. People will differ as to just how 'impossible' the doing of X really is, different principles and interests will pull in different directions: what is out of the question for A, B will do without a second thought.

If a doctor believes that he must never deliberately take life and so refuses to perform an abortion, even though the mother will die if the abortion is not performed, he does not see himself as causing the mother's death, rather he believes himself to have no choice. It is significant that such a man is often described as following the dictates of the divine law, or of his conscience, 'whatever the consequences', and that discussions of the problems raised by such dilemmas are discussions of whether absolutist moral principles which ignore consequences can be justified. The point again, is not that one has to be a consequentialist, but that the adoption of principles or values, or even ways of life or ways of organising society, which makes the prevention of certain sorts of harm by certain means 'out of the question', does not prevent the harm being a consequence of the maintenance of those principles or that way of life. If we decide that preventing particular harm by particular means is 'out of the question' we are unlikely to talk as though the harm were a consequence of our failure to prevent it. But the occurrence of such harm is the price we pay for the maintenance of our principles or of our way of life. We can never rule out the possibility of hungry people in the Third World, or even the victims of motor accidents in our own society claiming, with justice, that we are causally responsible for their plight because we decline to arrange things so that they may be preserved from harm.

To sum up we must emphasise a distinction that has been implicit in the foregoing discussion – that between A causing Y by his failure to do X and his bringing about of Y by his failure to do X. That is, the distinction between negative causation and negative action. We can state formally the difference between the two as follows:

a) *Negative causation*

A's failure to do X caused Y where A could have done
X and X would have prevented Y.

This definition of negative causation is, I think, strictly
true although, as many thinkers have observed, it seems
inappropriate, even silly, to talk of a man's being causally
responsible for everything and anything he might have made
different. There must be some reason for his interference,
some point to it. There must be some feature of the situation
that raises the issue to A's preventing Y by doing X. This
feature, whatever it is, will make it appropriate to talk both
of A's *failing* to do X, and of A's thereby *causing* Y. And this
will be so even where we neither expect nor require A to do
X nor to prevent Y. That we expect or require A to do X,
or that Y involves harm to human beings, are both features of
a situation that make it appropriate to talk of A's failure to
prevent Y by doing X, as causing Y. I don't intend this to be
an exhaustive list of the conditions under which A's failure to
do X can be said to cause Y. There may be situations in
which quite different features may give reasons for
interference and so make talk of causes appropriate.

b) *Negative action*

A's failure to do X with the result Y will make the
doing of Y a negative action of A's only where A's
doing X would have prevented Y and A knew, or ought
reasonably to have known this, and where A could
have done X and knew, or ought reasonably to have
known, this.

We must here emphasise the distinction (pointed out by
H.L.A. Hart)[41] between causal responsibility and 'moral
liability responsibility'; that is between causing some outcome and being liable, accountable in some way that makes
praise or blame appropriate. We are usually accountable for
some outcome because we are causally responsible for it, but
not simply because we are. It is only if the bringing about of
Y is a negative action of A's that his causal responsibility for
Y will raise the question of whether or not he might also be
morally responsible for Y. And of course, whether A is
morally responsible, whether he is to be held to account for
bringing about Y, will depend on a number of other

considerations, as indeed it would if he had brought Y about by positive actions. Among these will be the cost of preventing Y, both to A, himself and to society at large. Where more than one person could have prevented Y, or where Y's prevention, of its very nature, could only be undertaken by a large group or organisation, or even perhaps only by a large state, complex problems arise as to whether the responsibility for preventing Y is to be seen as individual or collective. The resolution of such problems will, of course, affect the question of who is to be *held* liability responsible for Y (but not the question of causal responsibility). The discussion of the problems of individual and collective responsibility we must postpone for the moment.

If the argument so far is roughly right, it presents us with a choice between only two consistent views about negative causation. We can deny that anyone is ever responsible for things he could have prevented or changed. This would go against many of our intuitions and common-sense judgments and would deny a whole realm of discourse long established and firmly entrenched both in our practice and in our habits of speech. The second alternative will be even less acceptable to many, for if we admit the concept of negative causation, if we allow that anyone is ever responsible for something he could have prevented or changed, then we must accept a drastic revision of our views about agency and responsibility.

Conclusion

In this chapter I have concentrated on showing that the view that we are causally responsible for the harm that we could have prevented is defensible, and what it amounts to. Chapter 2 argued that such harm, if it could be shown to result from the actions of persons may properly be seen as a form of violence. So we begin to see that the scope of man's violence to man is wide indeed. This conclusion has a number of important consequences particularly, as we have noted, for our views about agency and responsibility. But before going on to consider these, another nest of problems must be tidied up.

The account of negative actions given in this chapter helps, I believe, to demolish the thesis that killing is morally worse than letting die and also the view that there is an important moral difference between acts and omissions. More argument is, however, needed and this we must now provide.

Chapter 4

Killing and letting die

The most exhaustive philosophical discussion of problems concerned with negative actions has been of the difference between killing and letting die. The traditional and most widely accepted view is that killing is of its very nature morally worse than letting die. Or, to put this point in a more familiar way, to perform a positive act with the result that someone dies is morally worse than to fail to perform a different act with identical consequences. This I will call 'the moral difference thesis'.

We will start by looking at the famous and influential doctrine of the double effect.

The doctrine of the double effect

The doctrine of the double effect distinguishes between what a man foresees will result from his conduct and what in the strict sense he intends. A person intends in this strict sense both those things that he aims at as ends and those that he aims at as means to his end. But a person's actions may have a second, unwanted and unintended effect, an effect that may be foreseen but is in no way aimed at either as an end, or as a means to an end. The doctrine of double effect holds that where the bringing about of a particular result is absolutely forbidden, while we may not bring about such a result intentionally, the absolute prohibition may not extend to the bringing about of such a result as the 'second effect' of our intended actions.

The most widely discussed example in the voluminous literature about the doctrine of double effect is the so-called 'obstetrical example' (considered on p.34). In this example a doctor is faced with two possibilities: a pregnant woman in his care will die if she carries her child to term, when she is dead the child can be safely delivered alive by *post mortem* Caesarian section. Alternatively the life of the mother can be saved by the performance of an operation which crushes the skull of the foetus so that it can be extracted from the womb without danger to the mother. Those who believe that they must under *no* circumstances kill the innocent and who believe that this prohibition applies to the killing of the foetus, argue that the doctrine of the double effect shows that the surgeon must allow the mother to die and then deliver the baby alive by *post mortem* Caesarian. The rationale of this decision is that if the mother is allowed to die, her death is not part of anyone's plan, no one intends her death in the strict sense and, therefore, no one has broken the absolute prohibition against killing the innocent. Whereas crushing the skull of the foetus does involve the intentional killing of the innocent and is, therefore, forbidden whatever the consequences.

Leonard Geddes, in a gallant attempt to rescue the mother in such cases from the lofty sentiments of the absolutists, has produced the following somewhat oversubtle argument:[1]

The surgeon must remove the child from the mother's womb; the dimensions of the child are such that if the surgeon attempts to remove it without changing these dimensions the mother will surely die. He therefore alters these dimensions in certain ways. A necessary but quite unneeded and unwanted consequence of this procedure is that the child dies. Clearly the death of the child does not enter into consideration as a means to anything. So, in the relevant sense, the killing of the child was not intended by the surgeon, either as an end in itself or as a means to an end. Hence it is a mistake to think that the principle concerning the killing of the innocent applies to [this] sort of killing.

It would be instructive to conceive of a project which involved altering the dimensions of Mr Geddes in certain ways of which a necessary but quite unneeded and unwanted consequence would be that he is made exceedingly uncomfortable.

His response to such a proposal would, no doubt, help us to make clear the issues involved.

I do not wish to imply that the view that we do not intend the necessary and natural consequences of our acts is an implausible one. An example of Anthony Kenny's certainly seems to support it. Kenny points out[2] that when I get drunk this evening I know that I will have a hang-over tomorrow, but it would be ridiculous to say that I intend to have a hang-over tomorrow. Rather I think the conclusion to be drawn is that 'intention', which lends itself to such sophistical arguments, is not much help in determining responsibility or in distinguishing the moral quality of different actions with the same or similar consequences. It looks as though intention can be so narrowly defined as to yield any moral answer that is wanted.

It is not clear whether the doctrine of double effect is supposed to *explain* our response to certain difficult cases or to *dictate* what our response should be to such cases. The theory of negative actions developed in Chapter 3, and Geddes's sophistical distinctions show that we may bring about all sorts of evil which we do not aim at either as an end or as a means to an end. If the doctrine of double effect is supposed to explain the widespread feeling that it is worse to kill than to let die, by pointing out that this feeling is prompted by our judgment that it is worse to kill someone whose life you need to take for some purpose or other, than to kill someone whose death you do not need for any purposes of your own, then we would want to know why on earth we should make such a judgment. If on the other hand the argument just is that we *ought* to see that death as a first effect of what we do, is worse than death as a second effect of what we do, we again would want to see some argument as to why we should accept this.

One might feel intuitively that the moral difference went the other way; that there is something frivolous or gratuitous about killing someone for whose death one has no use. Far from being a worse person for aiming at their death, one is a better person for so doing, given that they are going to die as a consequence of your actions anyway.

We shall be looking in some detail at the many differences

between positive and negative killing to see whether any of
them have the sort of moral weight that could justify preferring one to the other. For the moment, however, our business
is with the doctrine of the double effect which locates that
moral difference precisely at the issue of the directness of
the agency involved, and where directness is understood in
terms of the intention with which the act is done.

Double effect and absolutism

R.A. Duff,[3] in a recent discussion of the doctrine of the
double effect, does his best to rescue it as part of a coherent
morality and ties it firmly to moral absolutism. According to
Duff, what matters to the absolutist 'is what I *do*; and "what
I do" is determined not just by what happens, but by the
intention revealed in my action . . . . His absolute prohibition
is against the intentional action of killing, not against the
occurrence, or the foreseen and avoidable causation of death:
it would indeed be absurd to prohibit *that* absolutely, since
for any prohibited outcome we would imagine a case in
which the outcome of any alternative is even worse.'[4] One
might think that to prohibit *anything* absolutely is absurd for
that reason, but I won't press this point here for it is just to
re-assert consequentialism in opposition to absolutism.

Duff then goes on to state that the absolutist's task is to
'show the sense that (this notion of agency) has, in particular
contexts, and to show how it is part of an intelligible moral
perspective of human life'.[5] This task is, he believes, 'simpli-
fied by the fact that we ourselves attribute a similar significance to agency. We draw moral distinctions between what
we intentionally do and what our actions foreseeably cause
or what we fail to prevent'. By his reference to the moral
distinctions that we draw here I suppose that Duff means
that we think it is morally worse to kill intentionally than to
act with the foreseen consequence that someone will die.
But this is a strange conclusion for Duff to come to for it
involves a comparative judgment and he specifically says that
it is wrong to suggest that the absolutist 'has weighed the
commensurable evils of killing and of not killing in a range of

cases and is now committed to a prediction about their relative weights in *all* possible or conceivable cases'. 'The Absolutist', Duff continues, 'is not concerned with the relative and commensurable evils of alternative courses of action: intentional killing is not an alternative whose merits and demerits must then be weighed, but something which we may not even contemplate as a possibility.'[6]

The absolutist doesn't want us to *judge* that positive killing is worse than negative killing, he wants us simply to *accept* that it is, lest, using our judgment, we come to the wrong conclusion. For, to be an absolutist Duff concludes 'is to see one's actions and obligations in the light of moral demands which transcend all purely human interests and in obedience to which we may never contemplate killing, however "foolish" in practical or Utilitarian terms this might be'.[7] But this doesn't simplify the absolutist's job in convincing us of the coherence of his morality, for it gives us no handle on his morality at all. The fact that we share a distinction, if we do, is no basis for conclusions about the intelligibility of the system of beliefs of which that distinction is a part. Assuming voluntary education, if I send my children to school because I believe it will improve their minds and you do so because you believe it will destroy their minds, I'm deluded if I see our mutual commitment to the practice of schooling as evidence of the intelligibility of this corner of your morality.

It is here that absolutism takes on a dizzying aspect. For if it transcends all purely human interests one wonders why it specifically concerns itself with 'killing' rather than, say, 'painting'. The question is: are we to be allowed to conjecture why just these demands are being made? Are we to be permitted to think morally about the content of absolute morality? If not then there can be no argument except perhaps about the respectability of the source from which the moral absolutes transcend. But if so, and we must, I think, think so, then we must ask why does the transcendent giver of morality concern himself with *killing*? If it is because life is in some sense valuable, then why on earth should lives that people wish to end be more valuable than lives which no one aims at ending? For so long as I want to kill you, I absolutely must not do it, you are safe. Whereas the moment I cease to desire your death I can become your executioner,[8] if only I do it as a second effect of some not absolutely forbidden project.

The reason that I think we must be able to ask moral questions about absolute morality is that it is only by doing so that we can put ourselves in a position to assess whether or not it forms 'an intelligible moral perspective on human life'. And the question that we must ask of an absolutism that makes the doctrine of the double effect central, is, how intelligible is a morality which recognises that human life is in some sense valuable, indeed recognises it as very valuable indeed, and yet is prepared to sacrifice literally any amount of lives so that one person shall not have to bring about the death of one other *intentionally*?

If part of the answer is that it is good *states of mind* that matter, not life itself, one must still wonder whether anyone is entitled to assume that there are no good states of mind among those who must be sacrificed to keep his own pure. Perhaps the only salvation for the doctrine of the double effect *is* if the agent assumes that the states of the minds he must sacrifice are all good and are likely to worsen, for then, if they die, they do so in a state of grace. This would be a rational way of responding to an absolutist morality which gave states of mind this sort of importance. As rational as the way some South American Indians are reported to have responded to their conversion to Christianity. On learning that 1 they were all sinners and, 2 all sinners risk damnation, they are supposed to have dashed out the brains of their just-born infants so that they should die in a state of grace before they had had a chance to sin.

The difficulty with intention

All this, of course, supposes that we can define 'intention' narrowly enough to distinguish deaths aimed at from those brought about but not aimed at. This is I think a big problem for the doctrine of double effect and before we leave Duff's account of that doctrine we should notice the difficulties that he himself has with this issue because they indicate fundamental problems with this approach. Duff begins his paper by noting, as we have already done, that Geddes's distinctions generate 'sophistical and unacceptable conclusions and he reduces both the [doctrine of double effect] and the absolute prohibitions it is meant to support to vacuity'[9] but Duff's account of the famous Captain Oates shares Geddes's fate.

Oates, Duff reminds us, 'walked out to certain death in a blizzard to give his friends a better chance of survival'.[10] If suicide is absolutely forbidden for the same reasons as is intentional killing, then Oates's actions are permitted by absolutism, whereas had he shot himself he would have sinned. Duff takes up the account:[11]

Death we may suppose is equally certain in either case, the
end aimed at − of bringing his friends to go on without
him which he knows they will not do while he is there
with them − is the same. But the means adopted are
crucially different . . . . For in one case they will go on
because he is dead and he intentionally kills himself, by
shooting, as a means to this. But in the other case . . .
he intends them to go on because they realise that he has
chosen to withdraw from the group; and to achieve this,
he needs simply to walk away.

Of course, he knows, and they know, that he will
certainly die; but this is now a consequence not a part,
of his intentional action . . . this logical gap between what
he intentionally does and his consequent death − is
important, not because it allows him or them to hope that
he will in fact survive (they had no such hope), but
because it shows that his intentions, and attention, need in
no way be directed towards his death, all he is deciding
to do is walk away; the rest is up to God.

This is not far removed from the sophistry of Geddes. Had Oates lacked the strength to remove himself from the group physically but possessed a revolver, he might have equally effectively disassociated himself by putting the barrel in his mouth, pulling the trigger and thinking, 'Whether I die or not is up to God.' Duff seems to realise this. He cites a stronger case against his view, of the man who throws himself on a live grenade to save his friends. If this man is not killing himself because the grenade 'might not go off' then, as Duff notes, if someone throws him on the grenade he is not being murdered for the same reason. Duff confesses he has no adequate answer to offer, and neither do I.

The difference between X killed Y and X let Y die

Jonathan Bennett, whose intuitions told him that letting die was every bit as bad as killing, attempted, in a now well-known article,[12] to get at 'what difference there is between killing and letting die which might be a *basis for* a moral judgement'.[13] Accordingly, he decided not to consider those cases of letting die which are also cases of killing (as where x knowingly lets y drink the cup that z poisoned) and concentrates on those *movements* which he supposes distinguish killing from letting die. Bennett's view is that the 'connexion between Joe's moving and the calf's dying' which is appropriate to 'Joe killed the calf' but not to 'Joe let the calf die' is expressed by:

> Of all the other ways in which Joe might have moved *relatively few* satisfy the condition: if Joe had moved like that the calf would have died.

And the connection which is appropriate to 'Joe let the calf die' but not to 'Joe killed the calf' is expressed:

> Of all the other ways in which Joe might have moved, *almost all* satisfy the condition: If Joe had moved like that the calf would have died.

Bennett's analysis is ingenious, and he concludes that his analysis of killing and letting die gives no basis for different moral assessments; but the analysis is susceptible to genuine, though bizarre, counter-examples. Joe is captured by a mad experimental psychologist who surrounds him with electrical sensors so that almost any movement he makes will be picked up by the sensors and connect a circuit electrocuting the calf in the next room. One or two of the possible movements will, however, when detected by the sensors, break the circuits and release the calf into a field of buttercups. Joe moves, connects the circuit, and kills the calf. In Bennett's view, this would be a case of letting die, since of all the other ways in which Joe might have moved, almost all satisfy the condition: if Joe had moved like that the calf would have died. And if Joe kills a calf, shoots it, for example, in circumstances such that the calf would have died almost immediately in any event, perhaps because it was diseased or because someone else had shot it as well, that would, on Bennett's view, be a case of 'letting die'.

In his paper 'On Killing and Letting Die',[14] Daniel Dinello produces some equally bizarre counter-examples to Bennett's thesis and goes on to provide his own analysis of the difference between 'x killed y' and 'x let y die':

(1)   x killed y if x caused y's death by performing movements which affect y's body such that y dies as a result of these movements.

(2)   x let y die if

(a) there are conditions affecting y, such that if they are not altered, y will die.

(b) x has reason to believe that the performance of certain movements will alter conditions affecting y, such that y will not die.

(c) x is in a position to perform such movements.

(d) x fails to perform these movements.

Dinello claims for his analysis that 'it is not obvious that the distinction as I have now drawn it could have no moral significance' and concludes in disagreement with Bennett, that 'whether or not an act is one of killing or letting die *is* relevant in determining the morality of the act'.

Three kinds of letting die

We can distinguish at least three sorts of case in which we might want to say that x let y die. The first is where x fails to do something he is capable of doing and which he knows will prevent y's death, and y dies. This is the sort of case which Bennett's and Dinello's analyses are attempts to elucidate and the sort of case which dominates the literature. It is important to bear in mind that where x lets y die in circumstances such as these, he will be causally responsible for y's death but may not be liability-responsible for it.

The second sort of case arises where it is not what x could have done to prevent y's death which is at issue, but what x could have done *to kill y*. Here the reproach is not that x let y die when he could have saved him, but that x let y die when he could have killed him. In a famous case a driver was trapped in the cab of his lorry following an accident. The lorry caught fire and it became clear that there could be no chance either of releasing the driver or putting out the fire before the driver was burnt alive. The driver asked a policeman to shoot him rather than let him be burnt alive and the policeman complied. In this case, had the policeman not killed the driver he would indeed have been guilty of letting him die. In this sort of case x will be causally responsible for y's death not because he was required to save y's life but rather because he was required to save y from a certain sort of death.

In the third sort of case, there is nothing x alone could have done to save y and yet we feel that he could have done *something*. Perhaps he could have tried to persuade those in a position to save y to do so. Perhaps he could have tried to persuade those about to kill y to desist or at least made some vigorous objection.

He could in any event have done something for y but as it turned out he just let y die, without so much as lifting a finger to help or comfort him. The point here is not that x is responsible for y's death in any sense, either because he could have saved him from death, or from a particularly horrible form of death, but rather that he just did nothing, or did not do enough; he just let y die.

Dinello provides what is supposed to be a counter example to the no moral difference thesis:[15]

> Jones and Smith are in a hospital. Jones cannot live longer than two hours unless he gets a heart transplant. Smith, who had one kidney removed, is dying of an infection in the other kidney. If he does not get a kidney transplant he will die in about four hours. When Jones dies, his one good kidney can be transplanted to Smith, or Smith could be killed and his heart transplanted to Jones. Circumstances are such that there are no other hearts or kidneys available

within the time necessary to save either one. Further, the consequences of either alternative are approximately equivalent, that is, heart transplants have been perfected, both have wife and no children, etc.

Dinello believes that it is clearly 'wrong to kill Smith and save Jones rather than letting Jones die and saving Smith' and concludes that this supports the thesis that there is a moral difference between killing and letting die.

If killing Smith is out of the question simply because his demise would involve *killing* — a positive act, rather than *letting die* — a negative act, then why do certain cases of letting die seem to be equally out of the question — these cases 'where x knowingly lets y drink a cup that z has poisoned' which Bennett describes as 'cases of letting die which are also cases of killing'? Dinello would have to reply that they only *appear* to be equally ruled out, to be equally bad, and that this appearance is shown to be illusory when we have to choose between killing and letting die as in the case of Smith; because in such a case we always find that we feel it more wicked to kill people than just to let them die. This view has a high degree of initial implausibility: if I am contemplating murdering my bedridden uncle I would have to be very sophisticated indeed to believe that sending him poisoned food was somehow morally worse than sending him no food at all.

Surely it cannot be that active killing is of itself obviously and necessarily worse than passive killing, that the employment of positive actions is always somehow more pernicious than the use of negative actions. On the view of negative actions already outlined, positive and negative actions share the same degree of causal efficacy. Both may be excused or justified in various ways, but both stand equally in need of excuse and justification, although, of course, the sorts of excuse relevant to each case may be different.

An argument from economy

We noted earlier (p. 26) Harold Orlans's[16] 1948 observation that:[17]

It is in the murder by neglect of decrepit old men that I believe the closest analogy is to be found with the death camp murders. The asylum murders are passive; the Auschwitz murders active . . . but otherwise their logic is the same.

In an exchange of letters with Harold Orlans, Dwight MacDonald,[18] then Editor of *Politics*, in which Orlans's paper first appeared, acknowledged that the cases were isomorphic insofar as they were both clearly murder, but sought to excuse the American murders not by emphasising that they were passive rather than active, but by arguing that it is less evil to murder people who are a burden on society:[19]

Both the death camps and our own asylums are indices of barbarism; but there *is* a difference — and one that favours American as against Nazi society — between letting sick people die through callous neglect and gathering up and exterminating at great expenditure of manpower and material, millions of people who are healthy (hence no burden to society) and politically passive (hence no threat to society's rulers) to equate the one with the other seems to me stretching things too far.

Even though MacDonald seems to think that murdering infirm activists at little expense is somehow *morally* less evil than murdering healthy, politically passive people at great expense, he is to be congratulated on seeing, at least, that passive murder is not morally better than *active* murder.

Positive and negative duties

Another and popular way of trying to account for the feeling, experienced by Dinello and others, that the conflict cases demonstrate that killing is morally worse than letting die is to do so in terms of 'rights'. This was the method once espoused by Phillippa Foot in a much cited article on the doctrine of the double effect. Although Mrs Foot has now modified her views they are still worth examining.[20]

Mrs Foot explains that initially she believed that the doctrine of double effect explained our response to these conflict cases, but that more recently she has come to believe that this conflict 'should be solved another way'.

Mrs Foot argued that our negative duties are much stricter than our positive ones and that we are accordingly strictly bound to avoid killing or otherwise harming other people, but are less strictly bound to bring them positive aid. On this view (that we may be consequentialists when giving aid, is all that is in question) if, for example, we can rescue a large group of people from certain death, or a smaller one from the same fate, but not both, we must choose to save the larger group. Here, according to Mrs Foot, our choice lies between 'allowing' many people to die, or only a few, so clearly we must 'allow' as few as possible to die. But where we can only bring aid by doing injury, we may be absolutists and resolutely decline to dirty our hands with the blood of hundreds of others. The moral difference between acting and refraining, on Mrs Foot's view, allows us to decline to do positive harm even where our scrupulousness puts us in the position of 'allowing' much greater harm to occur. And the moral difference exists, because to act so as to injure an innocent person violates his right not to be arbitrarily or unjustly interfered with, whereas to refrain from acting does not violate any right possessed by individuals.[21]

This division of duties into positive and negative according to whether the actions enjoined are positive or negative just serves to obscure the point of having duties at all, especially where the strength of the duty is supposed to vary with its mood. It is perhaps worth emphasising again that what we are concerned with here is harm to human beings, and in this connection there is just one duty, to avoid harming others if humanly possible. There are many ways of harming others; we may harm them by our actions or by our failure to act. The duty to avoid harming others has, then, both a positive and negative form. We have a *duty not to harm anyone by failing to perform actions which could be performed and which, if performed, would prevent harm happening to them*. This is the passive mood of the same duty which may be expressed in active mood as the *duty not to harm anyone by performing harmful actions the performance of which could be avoided*.

We are still left with the crucial question of why it is that we must refrain from killing Smith. Dinello thinks that we must not kill Smith because of the moral difference between killing and letting die. Mrs Foot believes that this moral difference is explained by the difference in force between positive and negative duties. She presents a pair of problem cases. 'We are about to give a patient who needs it to save his life, a massive dose of a certain drug in short supply. There arrive, however, five other patients each of whom could be saved by one fifth of that dose . . . .' Of this case Mrs Foot believes, 'we feel bound to let one man die rather than many if that is our only choice.' She continues: 'We can suppose similarly, that several dangerously ill people can be saved only if we kill a certain individual and make a serum from his body.'[22] As we have seen, Mrs Foot believes that the answer that we want in these cases in given by the fact that our negative duties are stronger than our positive one. Our duty to bring aid is weaker than our duty to refrain from injury, and so we may 'balance out' our positive duties to the five and the one, and with a troubled but not vitiated mind, share the vital drug among the five, leaving the one to die. We must on no account, however, renege on our duty not to injure people, and as we must not kill even one man to save however many more.

I will re-state Mrs Foot's examples to show most clearly the objection she might make to the assimilation of positive duties to negative duties in a way that makes both types of duty equally strict. We are to consider two men, A and B. A is dying for want of a drug, and B is perfectly healthy. We have no right to harm either A or B. To both of them we owe the duty to refrain from doing them harm either by performing actions which would harm them or by failing to perform actions which would prevent harm coming to them.

A can be saved by giving him 20 millilitres (our entire stock) of a wonder drug. However, there are two other men, W and X, who are also dying of the same disease as A, but who can be saved by only 10 millilitres apiece. We can either save A, in which case W and X will die, or we can save W and X, in which case A will die. Y and Z are also dying. They need new organs which healthy B has in abundance. All that is required to save the lives of Y and Z is for certain essential organs to be transplanted from B; B of course will die without these organs.

Now Mrs Foot would argue that we clearly ought to let A die and give the drug to W and X because, since we cannot save all three, we should save as many as we can, whereas equally clearly we should not murder B, even though by doing so we could save Y and Z. The reason that we let A die, but do not kill B, is on Mrs Foot's view simply that we owe B a stronger duty than that which we owe to A. Against my view she would argue that since I hold that the duty owed by both A and B is of the same sort and since, moreover, the same quantity of benefit is to be derived from the neglect of that duty, namely, the saving of two human lives, then clearly we should get the same answer in each case unless there is something different about the duties owed to A and B, or that there is some other difference between killing and letting die.

When faced with the plight of A, W and X, we have to decide what to do for the best and our choice is limited by the principle that we must not harm anyone by failing to perform actions we are able to perform which would prevent such harm. Clearly, there is no sense in which we are able to prevent the deaths of all three. We therefore have to choose between the three and I cannot see how we can avoid concluding that we must save as many as possible.[23]

What now of the plight of B, Y and Z? Again, our choice as to what to do for the best is governed by the principle that we must not harm anyone either by performing actions we could avoid or by failing to perform actions which we could perform. So why is it that killing B is out of the question in these circumstances? Why must we leave B completely out of the account and help Y and Z only if we can do so without harming anyone else?

Mrs Foot would reply simply that we have no right to harm B and perhaps that B has a right that we do not harm him, and that the fact that this negative duty is stronger than our positive duties to aid Y and Z must decide the issue. On this view it would just be wrong to say that our duties to Y and Z might also be negative duties, duties not to harm. But this attempt to explain why we are not entitled to kill B in order to save Y and Z is surely unacceptable.

It is clear that if Y and Z are dying before my eyes of snakebite and I have the antidote (of which there is a plentiful supply) and the competence to administer it, then if I fail to do so in full awareness of all the facts I have killed Y and Z as surely as if I had shot them. My failure to save them is a breach of the strictest of duties, the duty not to kill the innocent. If I now change this example so that the only antidote to the snakebite is 'extract of human heart', and the only 'spare' human heart around is in the live and healthy body of B, would we still wish to save Y and Z by giving them the antidote? Mrs Foot would argue that we would not and that my way of looking at obligation gives us no reason to prefer the life of B to those of Y and Z, since I hold that our duty towards all of them is a duty to refrain from doing harm. Mrs Foot's distinction, on the other hand, is supposed to explain why we are to prefer B's life to those of Y and Z. The reason is that our duty to B is negative and therefore strict, and our duty to Y and Z positive and therefore less strict.

But what if the only antidote to the snakebite is extract of human heart and the only 'spare' human heart around belongs to B who is alive *but not healthy*. He requires a daily insulin injection to keep him alive and is unable to administer it himself. I have plenty of insulin and can give him his daily injection. If I fail to give him his injection he will die and I can use his heart to save Y and Z. Now my duty to B is a positive duty, it is the duty to give aid to B in the form of insulin injections. It is a duty to save his life, not the duty not to kill him. But my duty to Y and Z is also a positive duty, also the duty to help them and not the duty to refrain from killing them. I suspect however, that the response of Mrs Foot and indeed of most people to this case would be to give B his insulin and regretfully to let Y and Z die. Our duty to Y and Z is a duty not to harm them if we can help it. So why in the circumstances of the present case are we supposed to think that we *can* help harming B and so *cannot* help harming Y and Z?

This example seems to show that we don't have the right to bring about the death of B by either positive or negative actions even though by doing so we might be able to save the lives of two or more other people. And it sorts well with our intuitions, for inasmuch as most people believe that we should not positively kill people and rob their bodies of organs to save the lives of others, so they believe we should not withhold vital drugs or refrain from necessary treatment of patients so that they will die thus releasing, as it were, their organs for transplants or, as in Mrs Foot's example, to make a serum. It is not, then, that we are forbidden to *kill* B, whereas we may let Y and Z die, but rather we may neither kill B, nor let him die, in order to save Y and Z.

But now this type of example does not do the work for which it was chosen by Dinello and Foot. For instead of giving us a contrast between killing and letting die and showing that an appeal to our intuitions yields the answer that in every case letting die is to be preferred to killing, it in fact shows that we prefer letting some people die rather than others.

But if this is so it raises another substantial difficulty, for might not Y and Z object to our preferring to let them die rather than B? Indeed on the theory of negative actions outlined in Chapter 3, our failure to bring about the death of B by either positive or negative actions and use his body to save Y and Z does make us causally responsible for their deaths. Most people would, I think, regard this conclusion as a *reductio ad absurdum* of our theory of negative actions, but perhaps this is because we are the prisoners of a particular moral system. At any rate, I intend to take this suggestion seriously and see where it leads us. To do so in the next chapter I am going to consider Y's and Z's case with some care.

Before we leave Mrs Foot's account of the difference between killing and letting die one last word on the question of 'rights'. I have been, and will be, concerned here with the question of what we ought to do if we believe that we should not harm others. It is certainly a fact that, because people have usually drawn a sharp distinction between positive and negative actions and given this distinction massive moral weight, in many of the cases where we have to choose between harming one person by positive actions and another by negative actions, the potential victim of positive harm will possess rights to be free from such harm that will not protect the potential victim of harmful negative actions. This may well make some moral difference to many of the classic conflict cases. The question I wish to press here is: can it ever make *enough* of a moral difference to warrant the sacrifice of even *one* extra life?

Chapter 5

The survival lottery

Let's suppose that organ transplant procedures have been perfected; in such circumstances if two dying patients could be saved by organ transplants then, if surgeons have the requisite organs in stock and no other needy patients, but they notwithstanding allow their patients to die, we would be inclined to say, and be justified in saying, that the patients died because the doctors refused to save them. But if there are no spare organs in stock and none otherwise available, the doctors have no choice, they cannot save their patients and so must let them die. In this case we would be disinclined to say that the doctors are in any sense the cause of their patients' deaths.

But let's further suppose that the two dying patients, Y and Z are not happy about being left to die. They might argue that it is not strictly true that there are no organs which could be used to save them. Y needs a new heart and Z new lungs. They point out that if just one healthy person were to be killed his organs could be removed and both of them be saved. We and the doctors would probably be alike in thinking that such a step, while technically possible, would be out of the question. We would not say that the doctors were killing their patients if they refused to prey upon the healthy to save the sick. And because this sort of surgical Robin Hoodery is out of the question we can tell Y and Z that they cannot be saved and that when they die, they will have died of natural causes and not of the neglect of their doctors. Y and Z do not, however, agree; they insist that if the doctors fail to kill a healthy man and use his organs to save them, then the doctors will be responsible for their deaths.

The rejection of Y's and Z's plea for life is based on the view that we must not kill even if by doing so we could save life, that there is a moral difference between killing and letting die. On this view, to kill someone, B let's say, so that Y and Z might live is ruled out because we have a strict obligation not to kill but a duty of some lesser kind to save life. The dying Y and Z may be excused for not being over-much impressed by this view. They accept that it is wrong to kill the innocent and are prepared to agree to an absolute prohibition against so doing. They do not agree, however, that B is more innocent than they are. Y and Z might go on to point out that the currently acknowledged right of the innocent not to be killed even where their deaths might give life to others, is just a decision to prefer the lives of the fortunate to those of the unfortunate. B is innocent in the sense that he has done nothing to deserve death, but Y and Z are also innocent in this sense. Why should they be the ones to die, simply because they are so unlucky as to have diseased organs? Why, they might argue, should their living or dying be left to chance when in so many other areas of human life we believe that we have an obligation to ensure the survival of the maximum number of lives possible?

Y and Z argue that, if a doctor refuses to treat a patient with the result that the patient dies, he has killed that patient as sure as shooting; in exactly the same way, if the doctors refuse Y and Z the transplants that they need, then their refusal will kill Y and Z, again as sure as shooting. The doctors, and indeed the society which supports their inaction, cannot defend themselves by arguing that they are neither expected, nor required by law or convention, to kill so that lives may be saved (indeed quite the reverse), since this is just an appeal to custom or authority. A man who does his own moral thinking must decide whether, in these circumstances, he ought to save two lives at the cost of one or one life at the cost of two. The fact that so called 'third parties' have never before been brought into such calculations, have never before been thought of as being involved, is not an argument against their now becoming so.

There are, of course, good arguments against allowing doctors simply to haul passers-by off the streets whenever they have a couple of patients in need of new organs. And the harmful side-effects of such a practice in terms of terror and distress to the victims, the witnesses and society generally, would give us further reasons for dismissing the idea; Y and Z realise this and have a proposal, which they will shortly produce, which would largely meet objections to placing such power in the hands of doctors and eliminate at least some of the harmful side-effects.

Killing the innocent

In the unlikely event of their feeling obliged to reply to the reproaches of Y and Z, the doctors might make the following argument: they might maintain that a man is only responsible for the death of someone whose life he might have saved if, in all the circumstances of the case, he ought to have saved the man by the means available. This is why a doctor might be a murderer if he simply refused or neglected to treat a patient who would die without treatment, but not if he could only save the patient by doing something he ought in no circumstances to do − kill the innocent. Y and Z readily agree that a man ought not to do what he ought not to do, but they point out that if the doctors, and for that matter society at large, ought on balance to kill one man if two can thereby be saved, then failure to do so will involve responsibility for the consequent deaths. The fact that Y's and Z's proposal involves killing the innocent cannot be a reason for refusing to consider their proposals, for this would just be a refusal to face the question at issue and so avoid having to make a decision as to what ought to be done in circumstances like these. It is Y's and Z's claim that failure to adopt their plan will also involve killing the innocent, rather more of the innocent than the proposed alternative.

The survival lottery

To back up this last point, to remove the arbitrariness of permitting doctors to select their donors from among the chance passers-by outside hospitals, and the tremendous power this would place in doctors' hands, to mitigate worries about side-effects and lastly to appease those who wonder why poor old B should be singled out for sacrifice, Y and Z put forward the following scheme. They propose that everyone be given a sort of lottery number. Whenever doctors have two or more dying patients who could be saved by transplants, and no suitable organs have come to hand through 'natural' deaths, they can ask a central computer to supply a suitable donor. The computer will then pick the number of a suitable donor at random and he will be killed so that the lives of two or more others may be saved. No doubt if the scheme were ever to be implemented a suitable euphemism for 'killed' would be employed. Perhaps we would begin to talk about citizens being called upon to 'give life' to others. With the refinement of transplant procedures such a scheme could offer the chance of saving large numbers of lives that are now lost. Indeed, even taking into account the loss of the lives of donors, the numbers of untimely deaths each year might be dramatically reduced, so much so that everyone's chance of living to a ripe old age might be increased. If this were to be the consequence of the adoption of such a scheme − and it might well be − it could not be dismissed lightly.

Suppose, for example, that inter-planetary travel revealed a world of people like ourselves, but who organised their society according to this scheme. No one was considered to have an absolute right to life or freedom from interference, but everything was always done to ensure that as many people as possible would enjoy long and happy lives. In such a world a man who attempted to escape when his number was up or who resisted on the grounds that no one had a right to take his life, might well be regarded as a murderer. We might or might not prefer to live in such a world, but the morality of its inhabitants would surely be one that we could respect. It would not be obviously more barbaric or cruel or immoral than our own.

A fatal exemption

Y and Z are willing to concede one exception to the universal application of their scheme. They realise that it would be unfair to allow people who have brought their misfortune on themselves to benefit from the lottery. There would clearly be something unjust about killing the abstemious B so that W, whose heavy smoking has given him lung cancer, and X, whose drinking has destroyed his liver, should be preserved to over indulge again.

Security

What objections could be made to the lottery scheme? A first straw at which to clutch would be the desire for security. Under such a scheme we would never know when we would hear *them* knocking at the door. Every post might bring a sentence of death, every sound in the night might be the sound of boots on the stairs. But, as we have seen, the chances of actually being called upon to make the ultimate sacrifice might be slimmer than is the present risk of being killed on the roads, and most of us do not lie trembling abed, appalled at the prospect of being dispatched on the morrow. The truth is that lives might well be more secure under such a scheme.

Individuality

If we respect individuality and see every human being as unique in his own way, we might want to reject a society in which it appeared that individuals were seen merely as interchangeable units in a structure, the value of which lies in its having as many healthy units as possible. But of course Y and Z would want to know why A's individuality was more worthy of respect than theirs.

Playing God

Another plausible objection is the natural reluctance to play God with man's lives, the feeling that it is wrong to make any attempt to re-allot the life opportunities that fate has determined, the feeling that the deaths of Y and Z would be 'natural', whereas the death of anyone killed to save them would have been perpetrated by men. But if we are able to change things, then to elect not to do so is also to determine what will happen in the world. We would be playing God quite as much if we left Y and Z to their fate as we would if we killed B.

Of course if Y alone could be saved by the killing of B we would be reluctant to play God, but this is not because it's wrong to play God, but wrong to do so *to no purpose*. In the present example we do have a reason to re-allot the life opportunities that fate has determined – we can thereby save an extra life.

Professor Anscombe has attacked the moral importance of saving more lives rather than fewer:[1]

> If there are a lot of people stranded on a rock, and one person on another, and someone goes with a boat to rescue the single one, what cause so far have any of the others for complaint? They are not injured unless help that was owing to them was withheld. There was one boat that could have helped them: but it was not left idle; no, it went to save that other one. What is the accusation that each of them can make? What wrong can he claim has been done him? None whatever: unless the preference signalises some ignoble contempt.

Professor Anscombe insists that a man 'doesn't act badly if he uses his resources to save X . . . *for no bad reason*, and is not affected by the consideration that he could save a larger number of people'.[2]

Professor Anscombe's view is certainly eccentric for it robs us of a perspective from which to criticise wasteful social policies, at least those which are wasteful of lives. But there are two alternative and equally catastrophic assumptions behind Professor Anscombe's position. I cannot improve upon Jonathan Glover's[3] ingenious exposure of these assumptions:[4]

Underlying this is the unstated belief that the time at which someone's life is in jeopardy is relevant to the moral importance of saving it. This curious assumption is a necessary feature of the position as we can see from consideration of some more people stranded on the rocks.

Suppose there are two rocks and on Monday the lifeboatman hears that A and B are stranded one on each rock. He has only time to go to one rock before both are submerged by the tide. Neither rock is harder to reach than the other. He knows nothing about the identity of A and B, only that they are different people. Here we might all agree that it is morally indifferent which rock he goes to. Now suppose a third person, C, is stranded on one of the two rocks on Tuesday. We may all agree that it is of some moral importance that the lifeboatman should rescue him. But, according to Professor Anscombe's view, if C had instead been stranded with either A or B on Monday, the prospect of saving him as well as one of the others need not have been considered of any moral importance at all. This will appeal to all those who think that saving lives consecutively is more important than saving lives simultaneously. (The alternative assumption is that the rightness of saving a life has nothing to do with any value placed on the life which is saved.)

Positive and negative actions again

Neither does the alleged moral difference between killing and letting die afford a respectable way of rejecting the claims of Y and Z. For if we really want to counter proponents of the lottery, if we really want to answer Y and Z and not just put them off, we cannot do so by saying that the lottery involves killing and object to it for that reason, because to do so would, as we have seen, just beg the question as to whether the failure to save as many people as possible might not also amount to killing. To put this point another way: the view that there is a moral difference between killing and letting die cannot be used in support of the alleged moral difference between killing B and letting Y and Z die because it presupposes such a difference.

Last-door arguments

An argument that has sometimes been used to support the doctrine that there is a moral difference between killing and letting die is that to kill someone is, as it were, to close the *last*[5] door on his opportunities for life, whereas any failure to prevent his death merely closes *one* door — not necessarily the last — on his life chances. On this view, to kill someone is surely and certainly to kill him, whereas to let him die is to act so that his death will *probably* result. But it is a question of fact in each case whether positive actions are a sure, or less ambitiously, a more probable, method of securing death than are negative actions. To draw again on an earlier example, it is a question of fact whether or not my bedridden granny will more probably die if I bring her poisoned food than if I bring her no food at all. I may miscalculate the dose and she may gain nourishment from the food in which it is concealed thus prolonging her life, whereas if I bring her no food at all she may be rescued, or manna may fall from Heaven.

So, in each case it will be a question of fact whether the last door has indeed been closed upon the life of a particular person. There is nothing in the difference between positive and negative acts which makes the one inevitably or of itself a more certain method of bringing about death than the other.

Self defence

To opt for the society which Y and Z propose would be, then, to adopt a society in which saintliness would be mandatory. Each of us would have to recognise a binding obligation to give up our own life for others when called upon to do so. In such a society anyone who reneged upon this duty would be a murderer. The most promising objection to such a society and indeed to any principle which required us to kill B in order to save Y and Z, is I suspect, that we are committed to the right of self defence. If I can kill B and save Y and Z then he can kill me to save P and Q, and it is only if I am prepared to agree to this that I will opt for the lottery or be prepared to agree to a man's being killed if doing so would save the lives of more than one other man.

Of course, there is something paradoxical about basing objections to the lottery scheme on the right of self defence since, *ex hypothesi*, each person would have a better chance of living to a ripe old age if the lottery scheme were to be implemented. Nonetheless, the feeling that no man should be required to lay down his life for others, makes many people shy away from such a scheme even though it might be rational to accept it on prudential grounds, and perhaps even mandatory on utilitarian grounds. Again, of course, Y and Z would reply that the right of self defence must extend to them as much as to anyone else. And while it is true that they can only live if another man is killed, they would claim that it is also true that if they are left to die, then someone who lives on does so literally over their dead bodies.

Side effects

It might be argued that the institution of the survival lottery has not gone far to mitigate the harmful side-effects in terms of terror and distress to victims, witnesses and society generally, that would be occasioned by doctors simply snatching passers-by off the streets and disorganising them for the benefit of the unfortunate. Donors would, after all, still have to be procured, and this process, however it was carried out, would still be likely to prove distressing to all concerned. The lottery scheme would eliminate the arbitrariness of leaving the life and death decisions to the doctors, and remove the possibility of such terrible power falling into the hands of any individuals, but the terror and distress would remain. The effect of having to apprehend presumably unwilling victims would give us pause.

Perhaps only a long period of education or propaganda could remove our abhorrence. What this abhorrence reveals about the rights and wrongs of the situation is, however, more difficult to assess. We might be inclined to say that only monsters could ignore the promptings of conscience so far as to operate the lottery scheme. But the promptings of conscience are not necessarily the most reliable guide. In the present case Y and Z would argue that such promptings are mere squeamishness, an over nice self-indulgence that costs lives. Death, Y and Z would remind us, is a distressing experience whenever and to whomever it occurs, so the later it occurs the better. Fewer victims and witnesses will be distressed as part of the side-effects of the lottery scheme than would suffer as part of the side-effects of not instituting it.

Common decency

One form of absolutist argument perhaps remains. This involves taking an Orwellian stand of some principle of common decency. The argument would then be that even to enter into the sort of 'macabre' calculations that Y and Z propose, displays a blunted sensibility, a corrupted and vitiated mind. Forms of this argument have been advanced recently by Noam Chomsky,[6] Stuart Hampshire,[7] Bernard Williams[8] and Jonathan Bennett.[9] The indefatigable Y and Z would, of course, deny that their calculations are in any sense 'macabre', but on the contrary are the most humane course available in the circumstances. Moreover, they would claim that the Orwellian stand on decency is the product of a closed mind and not susceptible to rational argument. Any reasoned defence of such a principle would have to appeal to notions like respect of human life (as Hampshire's argument in fact does) and these Y and Z could of course make comformable to their own position.

Rights

A particularly tenacious form of objection to the survival
lottery is that we have no *right* so much as to assault A, even
if we could thereby save any number of lives. Well, we may
well not have such a right, but so much the worse for us. I am
concerned not so much with what rights people happen to
have, but with what we ought to do. It may be that we
ought not to respect rights if the cost of doing so is this high
or, perhaps, that we ought to revise our system of rights.

J.G. Hanink[10] has set out an objection of this form in some
detail. Hanink accuses Y and Z of falling for an outrageously
sophistical argument, only to fall for it himself. I pointed out
that Y and Z can say that they did not intentionally seek A's
death, only his heart and lungs, and if A could live without
these that would be fine with Y and Z. Hanink's point is that
since the organs in question are *vital* organs, the link between
their removal and death is conceptual, not contingent, and so
in removing them Y and Z must intentionally seek A's death.
But then Hanink offers us the following case. Jones, Smith
and Robinson are confined to close quarters with one another
on a ship. Jones has a highly contagious disease which will
kill Smith and Robinson but not Jones himself. If Smith and
Robinson expel Jones he will die, but they will escape infec-
tion; if they don't, they will die and he won't. Hanink argues,
'Smith and Robinson cannot kill Jones in self defence. *For
Jones does not violate any right of theirs intentionally or
otherwise.*'[11] But, the absence in Smith and Robinson of
Jones's bacteria is a *vital absence*, just as the presence in A
of a heart and lungs is a vital presence. Can one really say
that one intentionally acts so as to communicate a deadly
contagion but does not intend the consequent death?

Hanink's real difficulty is that he does not see Jones
knowingly infecting Smith and Robinson with a deadly
disease as something he is *doing* to them.

If Smith and Robinson cannot throw Jones off the boat in
self defence, can they refuse to allow him on board knowing
that they will die if they do and that he will if they don't?
Jones has, after all, no *right* to come aboard.[12] Can thirty
people on a lifeboat refuse to let one more aboard if he will

sink the boat but now throw someone off for the same reason? Sure, they must choose the one to be ejected fairly, but that is what the survival lottery is for.

These are hard choices and hard cases, but I don't think a normative moral theory which sacrifices the lives of many to preserve the rights of one, can be too confident of a knock-down victory over its rivals.

Choice of victims

Lastly, a more limited objection to the survival lottery might be made, not to the idea of killing to save lives, but to the involvement of 'third parties'. Why, so the objection goes, should we not give Z's heart to Y or Y's lungs to Z, the same number of lives being thereby preserved and no one else's life set at risk?

Y's and Z's reply to this objection differs from their previous line of argument. To amend their plan so that the involvement of so called 'third parties' is ruled out would, Y and Z claim, violate their right to equal concern and respect with the rest of society. They argue that such a proposal would amount to treating the unfortunate, who need new organs if they are to survive, as a class within society whose lives are considered to be of less value than those of its more fortunate members. What possible justification could there be for singling out one group of people whom we would be justified in using as donors but not another?

The idea in the mind of those who would propose such a step must be something like the following: since Y and Z cannot survive, since they are going to die in any event, there is no harm in putting their names into the lottery, for the chances of their dying cannot thereby be increased and will, in fact, almost certainly be reduced. But this is just to ignore everything that Y and Z have been saying. For if their lottery scheme is adopted they are not going to die in any event, their chances of dying are no greater and no less than any other participant in the lottery whose number may come up.[13] This ground for confining selection of donors to the unfortunate therefore disappears, as does any which discriminates against Y and Z as members of a class whose lives are less worthy of respect than those of the rest of society.

It might be argued more plausibly that the dying who cannot themselves be saved by transplants or by any other means at all, should be the priority selection group for the computer programme. But how far off must death be for a man to be classified as 'dying'? Those so classified might argue that their last few days or weeks of life are as valuable to them — if not more valuable — than the possibly longer span remaining to others. The problem of narrowing down the class of possible donors without discriminating unfairly against some sub-class of society is, I suspect, insoluble.

Such is the case for the survival lottery. There seem to be good reasons for utilitarians to be in favour of it, and absolutists cannot object to it on the ground that it involves killing the innocent, for it is Y's and Z's case that any alternative must also involve killing the innocent. If the absolutist wishes to maintain his objection he must point to some morally relevant difference between positive and negative killing. The most likely candidate for something which might make this moral difference is 'intention'. An absolutist might argue that Y and Z intend the death of A whereas no one wishes to kill Y and Z. But Y and Z can reply that the death of A is no part of their plan, they merely wish to use a couple of his organs and if he cannot live without them . . . *tant pis*!

A fit, either of exaltation or of depression (to which those such as Y and Z whose philosophical deliberations are of the life and death variety are prone) has led Y and Z to underestimate some of the difficulties faced by their version of the survival lottery.

A fatal exemption re-visited

Conscious of the injustice of allowing people who have brought their illness on themselves to benefit from the lottery at the expense of the prudent who have led 'healthy' lives, Y and Z were prepared to exempt such people from the otherwise universal application of the lottery. The unfairness of killing the abstemious B so that W (whose heavy smoking has given him cancer) and X (whose drinking has destroyed his liver) should be preserved to overindulge again, weighed heavily with Y and Z. But the exemption they consequently proposed brings grave problems in its wake.

First, the difficulty of deciding whether or how far someone was responsible for their illness is overwhelming. The connection between various items of diet and diseases of various organs has been established and new connections are suggested almost daily. In addition to the sometimes fatal consequences of alcohol and tobacco, sugar, eggs, milk, butter, cheese and meat have all been cited as possible causes of disease. In addition to factors of diet, how heavy we are, how much exercise we take and of what type, where we live, the sorts of job we do — in short, the sorts of lives we lead — may all plausibly be shown to contribute to our state of health. Even if there were cases where we could be confident that a person had in no way contributed to their illness, could we acquire this confidence in time to save them? The meticulous investigation of the life and work of each citizen would, even if theoretically possible, be hopelessly time-consuming.

In the face of this there are two courses we might take. We could try to regulate every aspect of the lives of everyone, so that all unhealthy or risky practices were eliminated. This, even if it were possible and acceptable, would probably be self-defeating, since depression can also be fatal. Alternatively, we might decide that a certain amount of injustice was a price worth paying for the saving of large numbers of lives, and push ahead with the survival lottery despite the impossibility of exempting the careless. This raises a further difficulty over which the exalted or depressed Y and Z have been somewhat cavalier.

Would the survival lottery save lives?

One feature of the survival lottery as proposed by Y and Z makes its implementation less than attractive. This feature is the tendency of the lottery to lead to a gradual deterioration of the health of any society which operates it. This happens in two ways. The first is caused by the fact that since diseased organs are no use for transplantation, the computer would select only healthy donors, thus discriminating unfairly against the healthy (a point to which we will return) and also, and more crucially, gradually leading to a society in which those with healthy organs, and perhaps healthy living patterns, were weeded out. This would be re-enforced by the second way in which the lottery would operate to undermine the health of society, namely by removing disincentives to imprudent action.[14] For why should I curtail my smoking and drinking because they are unhealthy practices when my diseased organs can and will always be replaced. And since they are likely to be replaced from people who do not have the same bad habits as I do (indeed from people who do not have any bad, i.e. unhealthy habits) the survival lottery will gradually lead to a society depopulated of the prudent and populated by the imprudent. And thus to a society in which eventually it would be difficult to find suitable donors and thus both to a situation in which the lottery would cease to save many lives and also to one in which the healthy would live under virtual sentence of death.

Perhaps the last nail in the coffin of a society-wide lottery would be our fears as to its misuse. The lottery would be a powerful weapon in the hands of someone prepared and able to misuse it. Could we ever feel certain that the lottery could be made safe from unscrupulous computer programmers?

Choice of victims again

Y and Z, it will be remembered, were distressed at the prospect of the lottery being confined to themselves and others like them. When it was asked why Z's heart should not simply be given to Y or Y's lungs to Z thus saving the same number of lives, Y and Z replied that this would discriminate unfairly against the dying. But we can now see that a society-wide lottery would discriminate unfairly against the healthy. If this was merely the price that had to be paid for saving large numbers of lives it would have been a price well worth paying and one indeed that we often do have to pay already. Since wherever we have to choose between rescuing two different groups of people in circumstances in which we cannot rescue both, we choose to rescue the more numerous group. Indeed to believe that one should always save more lives rather than fewer, is always to discriminate against minorities.[15] Thus the principles of saving lives and of fairness are 'lexically' ordered in that we prefer to save lives and try to do so fairly, but where we have to choose between the principles, we choose to save lives.

Thus, if we have to choose between a society-wide lottery and one confined to the dying, where each lottery would save the same numbers of lives but where one was fairer than the other, we would have a reason to choose the fairer. But where both a society-wide lottery and one confined to the dying each involve discrimination in the selection of victims and neither offers a gain in the numbers of lives saved, then we have no reason gratuitously to swap one group of victims for another.

Moreover, because of the deteriorating effect that a society-wide lottery would have on the general health of the community, we have a good reason to confine the lottery to the dying. So Y's and Z's arguments against confining the choice of victims to the dying fail.

A modest proposal

We are left, then, with a more modest proposal, that in the event of the perfection of transplant procedures a survival lottery be instituted confined to the dying. Whenever two or more patients could be saved by the sacrifice of one then either straws could be drawn, or more fairly, a nation-wide scheme would be introduced to maximise the advantage. This could be a voluntary scheme and ought to prove attractive to the dying. For, in any group of three or more dying people where the sacrifice of one would save the other two and where all would die if the sacrifice was not made, then to fail to sacrifice one for two is to kill two people. So long as the choice of who to sacrifice is made fairly there would seem to be overwhelming reasons in favour of a survival lottery confined to the dying.

So we have to tell Y and Z that their original scheme was sound in principle but self-defeating in practice. But that a more limited version of the survival lottery, one confined to the dying, is both viable and imperative.

I say sound in principle because it is in a sense an unhappy[16] accident that only sound organs can be transplanted and that health is in large part contingent upon lifestyle. If, for example, a wonder drug were to be discovered that would cure any disease but that its only source was minced human brain and moreover that one brain would supply two or more doses, then so long as it did not matter whether or not the brains used were themselves diseased or what age they were, we could re-introduce the society-wide survival lottery. And all the arguments of Y and Z could then be re-introduced in all their pristine cogency.

The re-conditioning lottery

Alternatively and for good measure, if a process were to be discovered whereby we could extract human organs and re-condition them, then again the society-wide lottery could be resurrected. I am imagining circumstances which would allow for the extraction and re-conditioning of living human organs however far gone they were, but which do not allow for the survival of the donor. Donors would not have to be healthy, nor would they have to have tissue types compatible with the eventual recipients of their organs. Here all citizens could be in the lottery each time the lottery runs, including those who are about to benefit from the lottery and those who have recently done so. There would be no progressive deterioration in the health of a society which introduced it, nor would such a lottery discriminate unfairly against either the healthy or the sick.

Incentives to lead healthy lives and thus avoid a gradual deterioration in the health of society would be built in to this lottery. The imprudent as a class would not prey upon the healthy and all would have a reason to minimise their chance of being selected by the lottery, by minimising the number of times the lottery would have to be called upon to rescue the dying.

The arguments against confining this scheme to the dying would be those originally conceived by Y and Z. For these were only defeated by the discovery that the unconfined original lottery led both to injustice to the healthy and to a gradual sickening of society.

To be sure, it would discriminate unfairly against the victims, those picked as donors by the computer. But if it is bad luck to be a victim it is also bad luck to be dying of disease. What we should try to do is minimise the bad luck where we cannot eradicate it.

The re-conditioning lottery, however, allows for a less impartial alternative, but one more frugal of lives. If the gradual deterioration of the health of a society which operated it is an argument against the original survival lottery, then the gradual amelioration of the health of society should count in favour of a scheme such as that above, but which selects donors only from among the unhealthy *and* also the imprudent. This scheme would have the double advantage of gradually weeding out the unhealthy and replacing them with the fit, but also of re-enforcing healthy patterns of living. People would have the most powerful of incentives to adopt healthy ways of life and thus avoid placing themselves within the priority selection group for the health-promoting lottery. Lives immediately at risk would be saved *and* the general health of the community gradually improved.

But at what cost? First and foremost certainly at a cost to justice. The health-promoting lottery would re-introduce unfair discrimination against the unhealthy and imprudent. Second, and not far behind in importance, at a tremendous cost in terms of freedom. The pervasive inspection and control over the lives of all in the community which would be required for effective implementation of the health-promoting lottery coupled with the consequent disaffection and hostility of all those who would resent such controls, would prove formidable arguments against it.

In the face of such costs the gains might seem less attractive. The extra lives saved by the health-promoting lottery would not, of course, be those of people immediately at risk but rather of those of people who will not fall ill in the future thanks to the general improvement in health. We are inclined to give less weight to lives which will be saved in an uncertain future than to those in real and present danger. This latter point we will be looking at again in the next chapter.

But if we end this chapter preferring the magisterial justice of a completely impartial re-conditioning lottery to the rigours of its more frugal alternative, we should be aware that the cost of our preference is the lives of a number, perhaps a large number of once but future people.[17]

Chapter 6

The fate of others and our distance from it

Even if the most likely version of the survival lottery in terms of present medical technology would have to be confined to the dying, and the more fanciful but more economical re-conditioning lottery is still science-fictionally futuristic, we should be prepared to face up to the lessons that consideration of such possibilities can teach. The sorts of decisions envisaged by the survival lottery are already upon us and have been for a long while. If this is true, as I shall shortly show, the reaction that the survival lottery standardly meets is somewhat odd. Almost everyone to whom I have put the idea has sought immediately and often desperately, for objections.[1] The view that the survival lottery is clearly wrong and worse, corrupt, has seemed to many self-evident.

I want now to show that the moral features of the survival lottery and the sorts of calculation we might be forced by the perfection of transplants to make, are not the nightmares of a science-fictional future, but the familiar features of our own world. I will argue that it is better to face the fact that we may have to choose between lives and make these difficult choices in the best way we can, than to deny the existence of such dilemmas and kill arbitrarily.

The shortage of organs for clinical transplantation

The title of this section is also the title of a discussion document produced by a sub-committee of the British Transplantation Society and published on the 1 February 1975.[2] The terms of reference were to report to the British Transplantation Society on the following matters:[3]

a) How serious is the shortage of donor organs?
b) What are the factors responsible for the shortage?
c) To consider the law, the procedures adopted by coroners, criteria for establishing death, in particular brain death, and ethical matters concerning the care of the donor relating to the medical and nursing professions and the general public.
d) In the light of these discussions to recommend procedures for improving the supply of donor organs.

The need for the report is shown by the answer to its first question:[4]

The four transplantation surgeons present were in agreement that there was a grave shortage of kidneys for transplantation; 450 kidneys a year were being transplanted in the United Kingdom, whereas around 2,000 people a year needed transplants. It was difficult to establish the exact figure of those requiring transplantations, but it was felt that many patients were dying of kidney disease without the offer of dialysis or transplantation. As some transplants failed in patients who could subsequently receive second grafts, more kidneys were needed than appeared in most estimates. Several transplantation centres had virtually ceased work, and no centre was working to full capacity. The shortage of donor kidneys blocked access to treatment of new patients with chronic renal failure.

And the authors of the report conclude that the very serious shortage of donors could be 'completely overcome if even a small proportion of the potential cases were used. Thus some 6,000 fatal road accidents occurred a year. As each potential donor could usually provide two kidneys, these sources would be entirely adequate for all transplantation needs.'[5]

This does not mean that we would necessarily be able to save the lives of all those with kidney disease even if all those at present suffering had available to them cadaver kidneys. Roy Calne, Professor of Surgery at Cambridge, gives the following prognosis:[6]

In grafts between identical twins where there can be no rejection and the organ, coming from a live donor, should be in perfect condition, there is an 85% chance of the graft sustaining the patient's life at two years and the longest period of survival after operation is now more than 18 years. If a kidney is grafted from a blood relative who is not an identical twin, the figures fall to 70% and 15 years, and with a cadaver donor (in which case both rejection and the condition of the organ are likely to raise problems) the figure is 48% and 11 years.

But even a 48 per cent survival rate would involve a substantial saving of lives which are now lost.

For obvious reasons we must expect the vast majority of donor organs to come from cadavers rather than from live donors. And here there is a problem because it is crucial for the success of transplants that the organ be in first-rate condition.[7] The British Transplantation Society report notes that 'Though some organs can be used when death has been diagnosed by traditional means — namely the absence of spontaneous breathing *and* heart beat — the quality of the organ donated is very much better if taken while the heart is still beating.'[8] If we define death traditionally we are faced with the decision whether or not to kill moribund terminal patients who cannot be restored to normal existence in order to save the lives of those who can.

The authors of the report obviously regard this as too radical a proposal, for they recommend the alternative of redefining 'death' so that a person is 'dead' when it is 'established that he had suffered an irreversible cessation of brain function and was incapable of spontaneous respiration'. In *The Times* correspondence which followed publication of the report, John Mahoney SJ insisted that 'the basic ethical dilemma is whether one is justified in incurring the risk of taking the last vestiges of life from a potential donor to improve the life of a potential recipient.'[9] While I would state the alternatives rather differently from Father Mahoney, he is surely right to insist that we be prepared to face the fact that we now have opportunities to save the lives of people who can be restored to health only by killing those who cannot, those who can live on at best as vegetables.

We are guilty of a terrible moral cowardice if we shrink from recognising that a high moral tone costs lives. A frightening example of this occurs in the report we are considering. The authors' 'proposed code of practice for organ transplantation surgery' contains the following restriction: 'If available relatives objected to the use of the deceased's organs for grafting, even if it were established that the deceased himself has not objected, the relatives' wishes would be followed.'[10] It should be noted that the report does not add 'always provided that other suitable organs are available to the transplantation candidate'. The authors seem prepared to sacrifice lives to the caprice or superstition of the relatives of cadavers (if indeed one can be related to a cadaver, surely it is people to whom one is related?). It ought to be apparent to the authors of the report that this sort of clause is likely to result in the death of patients, just as Professor Calne feels that in a world in which transplants were routine it would become apparent that 'failure to inform the transplantation team of suitable donors would result directly in death of uraemic patients waiting for transplantation, for whom insufficient dialysis facilities were available.'[11] The moral must be that legislation is required to make mandatory the 'donation' of any organ from cadavers or from those diagnosed as irreversibly unconscious.

Mobile coronary care units

Professor J.F. Pantridge points out that[12]
40 per cent of the deaths from coronary attacks are sudden in that they occur within one hour of onset of symptoms (McNeilly and Pemberton, 1968 Brit. Med J. 3.139) and 61 per cent of the deaths among patients under 65 occur within this time (Gordon and Kannel, 1971 JAMA 215. 1617) . . . . Unfortunately, the usual median delay in hospital admission is over eight hours . . . . It is, therefore, clear that hospital coronary care units cannot affect significantly the community mortality from acute coronary attacks.
Professor Pantridge's solution to this problem is to set up mobile coronary care units, staffed by qualified medical personnel and run through the ambulance service. Pantridge

has been operating this scheme in Belfast since 1966, and other mobile schemes are operating in Britain in Brighton and Newcastle. The best results it seems have been achieved in Seattle.[13] Pantridge reports that[14]

the Seattle unit . . . has had remarkable success. In the last
year of its operation there have been 64 long-term
survivors among patients resuscitated outside hospital. If
this figure is applicable to the urban situation in Great
Britain some 3,000 lives might be saved annually.

This hopeful prognosis seems to be confirmed by an editorial in the *Medical Journal of Australia*[15] which sees a prospect of saving 3,000 lives a year in Australia if patients can be brought to coronary care facilities early enough.

If we accept for the moment these optimistic figures we can see that the survival lottery is already at home and roosting. For if mobile coronary care units are saving lives in Belfast, Newcastle, Brighton and Seattle, there are thousands of cities in which the lives that provision of such care would save, are not being saved.

We should note for the record that some doubt has been cast on the claims made for intensive coronary care. K. Astvad[16] and others report that[17]

a retrospective study of the mortality rate of acute
myocardial infarction [the blockage of (usually) the
coronary arteries] in two groups of patients treated
before and after a coronary care unit was established
showed no difference between them. Though it is
difficult to compare two series retrospectively so far
there are no well controlled studies to demonstrate clearly
the value of coronary care units.

This report prompted another doctor to write to the *British Medical Journal*[18] pointing out that a report in *Health Trends* for February 1974 'makes it clear that provision of adequate neonatal care, including intensive care in maternity hospitals makes a great deal of difference to mortality in newborn infants as it has also done to morbidity'.[19] And he concludes 'The moral as regards allocation of resources is obvious but it is not obvious that it has been drawn.'[20]

The very difficult problem about how to allocate scarce resources, which is raised by the champion of neonatal care, constantly involves all those concerned in decisions between innocent lives. It involves saving some innocent individuals at the expense of others who are left to die. Jonathan Glover[21] has pointed out that the Chancellor of the Exchequer 'in his annual budget normally either fails to increase the old age pension or puts it up by an inadequate amount. In either case it is predictable that a certain number of old age pensioners will not be able to afford enough heating in winter and so will die of cold.'

Alan Ryan,[22] in a preamble to a discussion of the survival lottery, makes a similar point about the allocation of scarce resources. Talking about Stephen Meurs, who died of starvation although social workers were aware that he was being neglected by his parents, Ryan outlines the consequences of trying at all costs to prevent even one such death:[23]

> We might very well find that the price of saving the marginal death of an infant was allowing the deaths of three or four elderly persons. For consider the obvious fact that our resources are finite, and the time and energy of our social workers finite also; at some point or other in the application of social service effort to the task of preventing death, we shall face a situation in which social worker hours applied to children's welfare will be social worker hours taken away from the welfare of, say, the ailing elderly. On a larger scale, the point becomes more difficult to deal with, but even more compelling. Stephen Meurs died of malnutrition; but many other children die in accidents, which might be prevented if, in the home, social workers had been able to go and instruct parents in unforeseen dangers, or, on the roads, local authority spending had been allowed on lighting or resurfacing or whatever. Now, when we say 'There must be no repetition of cases such as that of Stephen Meurs', we are in effect saying that two or three children must be allowed to be run over or scalded to death instead.

While decisions about the allocation of resources do naturally involve choosing between the infliction of positive harm on the one hand and negative harm on the other, they do involve our choosing between lives and it is important that we be sensitive to this and make the terrible decisions that face us in full knowledge of their consequences.

The raid on Coventry

In 1939 British Intelligence obtained through the Polish Secret Service a copy of the German cypher machine 'Enigma'. A team of cryptanalysts working at Bletchley Park succeeded in breaking the German codes and were thus able to supply the Allies with much advance information about Axis plans. As a result at 3 p.m. on 14 November 1940 the team at Bletchley Park intercepted a German signal which gave Churchill at least 5 hours' warning of the Coventry raid. F.W. Winterbotham, the man responsible for passing information from the 'most secret source' to Churchill saw the Prime Minister's dilemma like this:[24]

> If Churchill decided to evacuate Coventry, the press, indeed everybody, would know we had pre-knowledge of the raid and some counter-measure might be necessary to protect the source which would obviously become suspect. It also seemed to me . . . that there would be absolute chaos if everyone tried to get out of the city in the few hours available and that if, for any reason, the raid was postponed . . . we should have put the source of our information at risk to no purpose.

Churchill had to balance the lives that might be saved by evacuating Coventry against the lives that might be lost by endangering the source and thus cutting the Allies off from other information which might well shorten the war and save lives. Churchill's decision was, of course, complicated by the difficulty of actually achieving the evacuation of Coventry and also by the possibility of the postponement of the raid and, no doubt, by other factors as well, but clearly he was involved in sacrificing some lives so that others might be saved — not an uncommon experience in war.

Compulsory military service

Before we leave that terrible sharpener of moral issues, warfare, we should consider the most obvious parallel with the survival lottery — compulsory military service in time of war.

First we should note that the survival lottery is likely to be more frugal of lives than is the military draft. For, in most wars, of those drafted many die, whereas relatively few people will be needed to provide spare parts. Some people[25] have thought that while the draft may kill many it is not known with certainty who will die, whereas the survival lottery has a 100 per cent casualty rate among those chosen, a rate that would be quite unacceptable even in modern warfare. But this objection rests on a confusion, for the people 'drafted' by the survival lottery are not simply those *chosen* but all those *included* in the computer programme. Those who will be *chosen* by the computer are no more certainly known in advance than are those who will be killed in combat.

Wars are, of course, fought for many reasons, but it is far from clear that any of them are morally superior to the wish to save human life which motivates the survival lottery. We respect conscientious objection in wartime, but objections to the survival lottery on grounds of conscience would be hard to come by. They would have to be absolutist objections or objections to personal survival at the cost of the lives of others, but this latter is of course not a reason for objecting to the lottery as such, rather it is a reason to refuse transplants provided by the lottery if ill, and to volunteer for it, if healthy.

Those who believe that there is a moral difference between a society which operates compulsory military service in time of hostilities and one which operates the survival lottery might want to insist that in the former all the killing is done by the enemy, by people outside the society, whereas the victims of the survival lottery would be 'home killed'. But while we can understand the reluctance of people to kill members of their own society, it has been the argument of the preceding chapters that this is what they might be doing if they failed to institute the survival lottery, and also what they would be doing in sending soldiers to their deaths in a war. As Carolyn Morillo has said:[26]

> We would characterise the decision to have a military draft in this way: either we sacrifice some innocent soldiers or a greater number of innocent lives in our society will be lost. (In fact it has often seemed sufficient to balance lives with national survival, survival of a way of live, survival

of national prestige, etc.). If we accept such reasoning in this case, then why not in the medical case? Either we sacrifice a certain number of innocent donors, or a greater number of innocent lives will be lost.

Hostages

We are all too familiar with one practice of hostage taking: the dilemma facing police forces and governments has been whether to meet the demands of terrorists and so gain the release of the hostages, or adopt the practice of the Israelis and refuse to give in to terrorists. This, of course, may involve sacrificing the lives of present hostages, the justification being that to give in would make terrorism profitable and thus escalate the practice of taking hostages and risk even more innocent lives.

Road traffic

We have already noticed[27] that considerably reducing the permitted speeds on our roads would, in all probability, save thousands of lives each year. In both Britain and the USA speed limits were reduced during the fuel crisis and the experience in both countries was that there were substantial reductions in accidents. This cannot yet, with complete certainty, be attributed to lower speeds since there was also less traffic during the periods of reduced limits, because of the scarcity and increased expense of fuel. However, we perhaps have an argument for combining all three factors on a permanent basis and so save many lives that are now lost. The hostility that the survival lottery standardly meets appears a black irony in the face of our society's continued willingness to sacrifice citizens to circulation. As Carolyn Morillo remarked 'You never hear it announced as a matter of policy that "this year we plan to sacrifice 50,000 people to transportation".'[28]

Moral character and personal distance

Reviewing a series of cases of the sort we have just been considering, Lawrence Becker[29] makes the following comment:[30]

> What discussions of such problems typically ignore is the
> force of agent-morality considerations in assessing what
> the rational course of action must be. As La Rue puts it,
> 'The values we hold . . . can be used for our own self-
> definitions − to give a particular shape and meaning to
> our life. Furthermore, they can be used to represent the
> type of society in which we wish to live. If we return to
> the combat . . . example, we might note that men in
> such a plight might think it important to live on a "band
> of brothers" principle.' I would put the same point by
> noting that we have (rationally defensible) worries about
> the sort of moral character represented by people who
> propose to stand pat and let present victims die for the
> sake of future possibilities. One who can fail to respond
> to the call for help is not quite the same sort of character
> as one who can fail to maximise prevention.

Becker insists that there 'is a kernel of rationality in the
reluctance to identify, morally, the one who does wrong
"indirectly", "impersonally" with one whose wrongdoing
is very direct and very personal'.[31]

It is far from clear what weight Becker's rational reluctance is supposed to have because he concedes his lack of
confidence as to whether indirect, impersonal wrongdoing
is 'always (or ever) *less* culpable' than direct and personal
evil.[32] But the kernel of rationality is located in what Becker
calls the 'personal distance' of the agent. This distance has a
number of dimensions: 'spatial', 'temporal', 'cognitive' and
'intentional'. Spatial and temporal distance mean 'far away
and long ago' (or far ahead) and Becker explains:

> by 'cognitive distance' I mean the sort of intellectual
> 'pullback' which allows one to know what is going on in
> a general way without being forced to attend to 'details'.
> By 'intentional distance' I mean the sort of intellectual
> pullback which allows one to define what is being done
> as, for example, solving a complex problem rather than

solving a complex problem which will permit the development of a weapons system.

We will be discussing in Chapter 7 how 'the values that we hold' are related to our 'self-definitions' and the particular 'shape and meaning' we give to our lives. Becker's present point is, however, and despite the disavowals already noted, that it is rationally defensible to believe that people who need personal distance before they can perpetrate horrors are of better moral character than those who do not and, moreover, that this difference in the moral character of the agent gives us a rationally defensible reason for distinguishing positive and negative infliction of harm. This is because 'the tendency to distance ourselves is not always a defect, and the self-exploitation of this tendency for moral wrongdoing is less appalling than the behaviour of those who need no self-deception to do the same thing.'[33]

It is difficult to know quite how to respond to these sorts of considerations. In what sense are such people less appalling? A first reaction[34] might be that at least we know that people who need personal distance from moral wrongdoing are aware that it is moral wrong that they are doing. There is at least hope that they may in time find the moral courage to do what is right. This is a plausible if feeble line to take although, like Becker, I cannot see that it affects their responsibility for their wrongdoing. The trouble is, it is not only wrongdoing from which we seem to need to be distanced. Becker mentions that 'anaesthesia and the sheets which drape a patient's body' perform the same important distancing function for the surgeon but here there is no question of wrongdoing. It begins to look as though this important psychological fact (if it is one) has less to do with moral character than something we might euphemistically call 'general personal hygiene'. We dislike messy or dirty jobs, we require personal distance from the task of cleaning up excrement, but this does not reflect our moral character but our fastidiousness. Perhaps the idea of keeping blood off our hands has less to do with morality than with some primitive feelings about cleanliness or purity?[35] This is, of course, speculation but it is difficult to see how this sort of thing could cut morally. It may be that we do *feel* differently about people who need distance but whether these are *moral* feelings is far from clear. We will be returning to this point in the next chapter but for the present we can conclude that while personal distance may commonly be employed to shield people from having to face the consequences of their conduct, this is just a sort of bad faith.

It is a no more rationally defensible way of morally distinguishing between positive and negative actions or direct and indirect wrongdoing, than is the method employed by Sir Robert Brakenberry in Shakespeare's *Richard III*. He knew very well that the murderers had come from the Duke of Gloucester expressly to kill Clarence but on receiving their commission he says:[36]

I am in this commanded to deliver
The noble Duke of Clarence to your hands:
I will not reason what is meant hereby,
Because I will be guiltless of the meaning.

The reason of course that Brakenberry will not reason is because he already has reasoned what it means and is guilty of the meaning.

Uncertainty distance

Although personal distance does not give us a way of morally distinguishing the indirect infliction of harm from more 'personal' harmful involvement with our fellows, in all the cases we have been considering probability plays an important role. Even in the survival lottery one cannot be absolutely certain that the transplant patients will live, though the risk is clearly worth taking as it is in quite simple current surgery. But with current kidney transplants, of course, the risk is greater and so we have to calculate the probable number of lives we can save if we allocate appropriate resources. Similarly with cardiac ambulances. In the war-time examples the probabilities are even harder to calculate: weighing such imponderables as the number of lives that may be saved by making sure that we protect the enigma source against the number that might be saved by evacuating Coventry (bearing in mind that the source may survive the evacuation of

Coventry), numbs the conscience. In the road traffic cases we have the added complication of uncertain statistics.

Carolyn Morillo has suggested that we call the distancing effect occasioned by our uncertainty about the precise consequences of rival policies 'probability distance'.[37] This feature does seem to have some moral weight because although as we have seen[38] there is nothing necessarily more uncertain about the consequences of negative actions rather than positive actions, our knowledge that good or bad consequences of either positive or negative actions are only more or less probable, makes us less willing to take difficult decisions.

Now in the straightforward cases where we know with reasonable certainty that particular measures − reducing maximum speed limits on roads, allocating resources to medical care, giving money to famine relief − will save lives, although we are uncertain as to precisely how many lives can thereby be saved, and precisely who those saved will turn out to be we should not let this uncertainty come between us and the people we can save. Perhaps it would be better to call the numbing effect of this sort of 'distance' 'uncertainty distance'. But there is a sort of probability distancing that does seem to carry some moral weight and this we might with more clarity call 'probability distance'.

Probability distance

Considering the common conflict between rescue and prevention Becker notes that 'we (and mine owners) will typically spare no expense to rescue trapped miners but hedge at spending the same money taking preventative measures − even if it is demonstrable that the preventive action maximises the number of lives saved.'[39] Becker goes on to say that 'rationality, here, seems again to dictate a "hard-line" approach .... Maximise the number of lives to be saved; and if that means − for economic or other reasons − that one cannot both rescue and prevent, then prevent.'[40] Becker does not, of course, believe that we should in these circumstances prevent, for reasons similar to those of Bernard Williams and Jonathan Bennett which we shall be considering in Chapter 7. Our present concern is with the role of probability in such cases.

Does rationality or even morality dictate that we take what Becker calls a hard-line in such cases? We do I think feel, as does Becker, that in his mine accident case we will want to save the trapped men. But if to do so we have to spend money that is allocated to safety measures which we know maximise the numbers of lives saved, could we justify so doing? Perhaps we can point to a moral difference here (one which, of course, has nothing to do with the distinction between positive and negative actions since we have to choose between failing to save present victims as against failing to save probable future victims). This moral difference can best be revealed by concentrating our attention on the *degree* of harm to be imposed on present victims and contrasting this with the degree of benefit to be conferred on the remaining miners. By failing to rescue the present victims we bring about their deaths whereas by letting them die and putting in train the safety measures, we confer on the other surviving miners, let's say, a 5 (or 25) per cent decrease in the risk of fatal injury.

The argument is one from fairness. It seems unfair to buy with the lives of their comrades, a *slightly* decreased risk of fatal injury for the rest of the mining community. We can contrast this case with the survival lottery in which the lives of two or more real and present people are purchased with the life of one other and the risk is evenly distributed. Here the burden imposed, the taking of one life, is commensurate with the degree of benefit conferred, the saving of two or more lives. Similarly in the case of famine relief. Real and present victims are saved by placing a, perhaps considerable, burden on members of richer communities. But still the burden is, one would think, acceptable given the benefit to be derived.

This way of dealing with Becker's case would give us a way of coping with another sort of case which might at first sight seem to raise difficulties for the view of responsibility I have been developing.

Hostages

What would be the argument against, say, a government's taking terrorist hostages and threatening to kill them one by one until the terror campaign stopped, if the best calculation was that such a policy would stop the bombing and effect a net saving of life? Most of us would feel that we ought not to countenance such a policy, but why not? Not at any rate just because it involves killing to save life for as we have seen we ought not to believe that that is sufficient reason.[41] The argument from fairness seems to offer a way out, because the burden to be placed upon the hostages is not commensurate with the benefit to be gained by the rest of the community. They stand to lose their lives whereas the rest of us will gain at best a slightly diminished chance of being killed by terrorist bombs. There is no one to whom one could point and say *he* will be saved if we kill a hostage.[42]

This is a tempting argument but consider the following case: 100,000 prisoners of war are collected in a camp; the commandant, for reasons of his own, wishes to demonstrate his powers; he tells the prisoners' senior officer that unless he will shoot a particular man, ten others will be chosen at random and shot. If we apply the same perspective on this case we have to ask what amount of harm does he do to any of the other prisoners commensurate with the harm done to the wretched man waiting to be shot? Each of the others has imposed on him only a relatively small percentage chance of being killed whereas the 'trapped' man will suffer death. Of course, if the senior officer refuses, ten will be chosen and then all the risk that was previously spread through the community crystallises on them. But this is what happens in the mining case when, because safety measures have not been taken, the inevitable disaster occurs.

These sorts of cases have unreality about them and we will be looking at some of them again in Chapter 7. We instinctively, and probably wisely, mistrust people like the commandant. We can't imagine how we might be convinced that killing hostages would deter terrorists[43] and we, of course, demand that the probability of the future disasters' occurring be of a very high order before we will sacrifice present lives in order to avert it. But if we did have to choose in some hard case we should not allow the distorting effect of probability distance to mask the nature of the decisions which face us or rob us of the will to make hard choices. What we must do is decide what our priorities are and, if we believe in saving lives, then we should act in the way best calculated to do so.

The difficulties of probability distance were precisely those which preoccupied Shakespeare's Brutus when weighing up whether or not he should assassinate Caesar, he convinces himself by reasoning:[44]

That lowliness is young ambition's ladder,
Whereto the climber upwards turns his face;
But when he once attains the upmost round,
He then unto the ladder turns his back,
Looks in the clouds, scorning the base degrees
By which he did ascend. So Caesar may:
Then, lest he may, prevent. And, since the quarrel
Will bear no colour for the thing he is,
Fashion it thus; that what he is, augmented,
Would run to these and these extremities;
And therefore think him as a serpent's egg
Which, hatch'd, would, as his kind, grow mischievous,
And kill him in the shell.

Chapter 7

Integrity, sympathy and negative responsibility

There have been two recent and powerful attempts to counter the theory of negative responsibility we have been exploring. The philosophers concerned are Bernard Williams and Jonathan Bennett and their contributions to the debate are important and require separate and detailed consideration.

Williams

Bernard Williams's essay, *A Critique of Utilitarianism*,[1] argues against consequentialism[2] largely by indicating ways in which a certain view of moral problems and dilemmas reveals the inadequacy of utilitarian solutions. Williams's positive account of how moral problems are to be treated and of the ways in which crucial decisions are to be arrived at is presented as part of his attack on negative responsibility and so we can both defend negative responsibility and explore Williams's account of moral decision making at the same time. I should add that I have no wish to defend the version of utilitarianism that is the chief object of Williams's scorn; the legions of the faithful will no doubt rally to its aid; rather I seek to play Williams's part and attack another form of dogma which is fast taking over from utilitarianism its role as a piece of machinery for providing quick solutions to moral problems.

101

Integrity and commitment

Williams introduces and explains the essential connection between consequentialism and negative responsibility as follows:[3]

> It is because consequentialism attaches value ultimately to states of affairs, and its concern is with what states of affairs the world contains, that it essentially involves the notion of negative responsibility: that if I am ever responsible for anything, then I must be just as much responsible for things that I allow or fail to prevent, as I am for things that I myself, in the more everyday restricted sense, bring about. Those things also must enter my deliberations as a responsible moral agent on the same footing. What matters is what states of affairs the world contains, and so what matters with respect to a given action is what comes about if it is done and what comes about if it is not done, and those are questions not intrinsically affected by the nature of the causal linkage, in particular by whether the outcome is partly produced by other agents.

Consequentialism thus holds that there are two ways of making events occur in the world: one is by positive actions, doing things with the result that these events occur, and the other is by negative actions, failing to do things with the result that these events occur. For those who wish to do so, the obvious ways to criticise the negative responsibility thesis are either to attack the causal linkage between inaction and consequence, and to claim that it is somehow more tenuous than that between action and consequence, or to 'discredit it by insisting on the basic moral relevance of the distinction between action and inaction'. We have already examined the difficulties involved in this expedient. Williams, interestingly, chooses neither of these two methods. The latter he discounts as 'unclear both in itself and in its moral applications, and the unclarities are of a kind which precisely cause it to give way when, in very difficult cases, weight has to be put on it'. Neither does he attack the causal linkage (except at one crucial point which I shall examine in due course) but rather assumes it. Instead he deploys an argument designed either to justify our causing harm by our negative actions in certain circumstances, or at least to defend our right to do so in these circumstances. It is this argument that I shall now examine.

The argument from integrity

The kingpin of the argument that Williams deploys against the negative responsibility thesis is the special and necessary value that each person must place upon his own integrity. For Williams a person's integrity is bound up with a class of projects to which the individual is particularly committed.[4]

How can a man as a utilitarian agent come to regard as one satisfaction among others, and a dispensable one, a project or attitude round which he has built his life, just because someone else's projects have so structured the causal scene that that is how the utilitarian sum comes out? The point is that he is identified with his actions as flowing from projects and attitudes which in some cases he takes seriously at the deepest level, as what his life is about . . . . It is absurd to demand of such a man, when the sums come in from the utility network which the projects of others have in part determined, that he should just step aside from his own project and decision and acknowledge the decision which utilitarian calculation requires. It is to alienate him in a real sense from his actions and the source of his action in his own convictions.

Williams takes for granted our nodding assent that indeed a man cannot step aside from his own projects to obey a utility machine which has been programmed by the projects of others. He reinforces his claim that a man, in some sense of the word, cannot dispense with his commitments, by suggesting that he has a right to defend his integrity, and by demonstrating that the categorical imperatives of utilitarianism constitute, in some circumstances, a fundamental attack on this integrity. We must concede at once that it would be absurd to demand of a man that he sell his soul to the utility machine, binding himself to throw over his own projects and deeply held attitudes wherever and whenever some slight gain for utility might thereby be achieved. And it might even be true that in some sense a man literally cannot, in the comprehensive way that utility demands, abdicate the direction of his own life and still keep the autonomy and integrity that give his life coherence, that make him an individual. But now how much of the thesis of negative responsibility have Williams's arguments demolished?

The first thing to note is that his weaponry is of rather heavy calibre and does not enquire too closely into the identity of its victims. He has produced a general argument to show that maintenance of integrity necessarily involves a certain degree of insensitivity to the needs or wants or to the happiness of others. But this attacks positive quite as much as negative responsibility. If it is absurd to demand of a man that he abandon his projects because someone has so structured the causal scene that a greater utility lies in his doing something else, then it is equally absurd to demand of him that he abandon a project which directly involves the same amount of disutility. Remember, we are talking about projects and attitudes that a man 'takes seriously at the deepest level, as what his life is about'; it would be as absurd to demand that a man abandon projects as important as these if some fractional general disutility were directly involved, as it would be if an equally small general disutility stemmed simply from his failing to do something else. If Williams wishes to demolish negative responsibility alone he must undermine its foundations, either by attacking the causal linkage, or by defending some sort of moral difference thesis, neither of which he in fact does, with the exception already noted but yet to be discussed.

While it may be true that a man cannot sell his soul wholesale to the utility network, it is not true that in any particular case he cannot sacrifice his projects to utility. To put this point in the language of negative responsibility: a man can come to regard his deeply held projects as dispensable when circumstances, even circumstances determined by others, force on him, or provide him with, the opportunity to prevent serious harm. So that in any case worth discussing it will not be true that a man cannot in any sense of the word, choose to abandon his projects. What he will have to do is choose whether to abandon them or not.

So we are left with the weaker position which argues not that we cannot abandon our projects when to do so would prevent harm, but that we need not do so. Now if this means that we need not necessarily or automatically abandon our projects whenever by our doing so a net increase in general utility could be obtained, then again we can concede the point. For again to do so would be to abdicate the direction of our lives to an extent that would rob us of the autonomy and integrity that give our lives their coherence and individuality. We must be clear that even here Williams's argument does not cut off negative responsibility. His argument does not show that we are not responsible for the harm that we fail to prevent, only that there are cases in which we are justified in not preventing it. The crucial questions are: which are these cases, and how are we to decide which they are? And again, in any cases in which the harm we might prevent is sufficiently serious to make us even so much as think about whether to prevent it or not, then we must surely ask ourselves whether there are considerations of sufficient moral weight to justify our not trying to prevent it. But it is just this sort of question which it seems that Williams wishes to protect us from having to ask. The special and necessary moral weight which he attaches to our integrity is supposed to relieve us from the necessity of balancing projects with which we are 'more deeply and extensively involved' against the harm which by abandoning them we could prevent. But how can anyone even remotely interested in doing the right thing in a given situation avoid this sort of calculation?

To recapitulate: negative responsibility holds that I am just as responsible for things that I allow or fail to prevent as I am for things that I myself, in the more everyday restricted sense, bring about. Nothing that Williams says damages this thesis. At most his arguments show that there are cases, perhaps many cases, where we are justified in, or can be forgiven for, occasioning some harm to others. But this is not news, and it applies as much to harm for which we are positively responsible as it does to harm for which we are negatively responsible; or if it does not, nothing Williams says shows that it does not.

As an attack on utilitarianism, Williams's argument from integrity has some success. He is persuasive in claiming that we cannot or need not automatically abandon our deeply held projects whenever any increase in general utility could thereby be obtained. But this leaves all the crucial questions unanswered. What we need to know is how far his argument from integrity is supposed to justify our being responsible for harm to others in any particular case. If a man is committed to his work or to his wife can he, while sitting at his desk involved in some vital calculation or by her side engaged in a crucial quarrel, ignore the cries of a child drowning in the pond outside? Williams goes no way towards persuading us that our integrity is of such overriding importance as to justify our not bothering to decide in any particular case whether our project is sufficiently important for us to pursue it at the cost of the harm, which by abandoning it, we could prevent, and again, this is just the sort of calculation that Williams wants to short-circuit. Irritatingly, when Williams gets down to cases he does not employ his argument from integrity at all, but rather offers some very different suggestions.

Negative responsibility: Williams's examples

Williams provides two fascinating and complex cases, but their fascination and complexity render the prospect of drawing any clear conclusions somewhat shady. It is clear that Williams values these cases primarily as counter-examples to utilitarianism; and they may well be, but one at least is also a counter-example to Williams's own argument from integrity. Williams seems to realise this, for he produces a new suggestion to accommodate this case, a suggestion moreover that puts morality beyond the scope of rational debate. These are the cases:[5]

1   George, a research chemist with a wife and small
children, cannot find a job. A friend can procure for
him a job at a chemical and biological warfare
establishment. The job is not to George's taste but if
George does not take the job a zealous contemporary
will. What should George do?

2   Jim finds himself in the central square of a South
American town. Twenty Indians are about to be executed,
but the captain of the soldiers (call him Pedro) offers Jim
this alternative: either Jim can kill one of the Indians
with his own hand and the others will be allowed to go
free, or, if he refuses, all twenty will be shot. What should
Jim do?

In George's case we are to judge that the utilitarian answer
is that he should take the job, thus providing for his family
and enabling him to slow down or foul up research, maximis-
ing utility all round. The alternative, sticking to his principles
and preserving his integrity, leaves himself out of work, his
family unprovided for, and an unprincipled maniac pushing
ahead with inhuman research. In the second case the utilitarian answer is more obvious. Jim should kill one man to save
nineteen. Jim's dilemma stems from his unwillingness to kill
anyone and from his distaste for being dragged willy-nilly
into an unsavoury situation of someone else's making, in
which he must choose between alternatives equally repugnant
to him.

Williams concludes that it is not hard to see that in George's
case, viewed from the perspective of integrity, the utilitarian
answer would be wrong. Here I agree with Williams though
not entirely for his reasons. Williams's reasons presumably are
that George simply *cannot* sacrifice his integrity, his plans for
his own life, the sort of career he wants and the sort of work
he wants to do, just because the utilitarian calculating machine
dictates that particular answer. This seems right but only
because George does not have sufficient reason to abandon
his own projects in favour of those of his friend. In order to
maximise utility George will have to work steadily for the
chemical and biological warfare establishment. Steadily
because if he is thrown out for bad work or for throwing
spanners in the works, a more zealous person will be employed
who will push ahead with the research and George's sacrifice
will be wasted. George is then faced with a lifetime of work
that is for him soul destroying and the gains are far from
clear. It is unlikely that he will be able to do much to slow
down the research without being replaced or by-passed and
even more unlikely that he will be able to reform or change

the direction of the research by exerting moral pressure – he will surely be in the position of the man who tried to reform the Nazi SS from the inside! And then again the weapons may never be perfected and if they are they may never be used. George is being asked to work his whole life away in an institution and for a cause he finds morally repugnant for highly speculative advantage to the cause of peace and sanity. It is even unlikely that the course recommended by his friend is the best from the point of view of utility. Probably greater effect could be achieved by his devoting himself to political activity in his spare time or in accepting the job and then, say, resigning in a blaze of publicity exposing the shocking things he found going on in the laboratory.

But let us grant that utility might just be on the side of George's taking the job. There is his family to consider, and we can, I suppose, imagine that it might on balance be safer for mankind, and so consistent with utility, if, as a precaution, men like George worked in places like chemical and biological warfare establishments. And in such a case I think Williams is right in supposing that most people would agree that George need not (i.e. it is not the case that he ought to) take the job; after all, the harm that George, by taking the job, might prevent is itself highly speculative.

But now compare Jim's case. Nineteen or twenty lives are definitely and immediately at risk and the action required to save nineteen of them is not the work of a lifetime but of a second or two. Williams clearly senses the difference between the cases for he thinks that the utilitarian judgment about Jim's case is probably the right one.[6]

> The immediate point of all this is to draw one particular contrast with utilitarianism: that to reach a grounded decision in such a case should not be regarded as a matter of just discounting one's reactions, impulses and deeply held projects in the face of the pattern of utilities, nor yet merely adding them in – but in the first instance of trying to understand them.

Here again I agree with Williams, but he does not appear to agree with himself. One would expect him to go on to give an account of how Jim's integrity, his various commitments, and his deeply held projects and beliefs might weigh with him in coming to a grounded decision: and of whether the sort of weight these considerations might have would be sufficient to counter-balance the nineteen lives in the scales with them. But Williams does not do this, for the very good reason that one cannot imagine what commitments Jim might have that would warrant the sacrifice of nineteen lives. What Williams does is throw out a number of suggestions that he believes Jim's case and others involving negative responsibility will 'have to take seriously'. But before looking closely at these suggestions we must, as promised, consider Williams's attempt to attack the causal connection between inaction and consequence. It comes in the context of Jim's case:[7]

> For Pedro's killing the Indians to be the outcome of Jim's refusal, it only has to be causally true that if Jim had not refused, Pedro would not have done it.
>
> That may be enough for us to speak, in some sense of Jim's responsibility for that outcome, if it occurs; but it is certainly not enough, it is worth noticing, for us to speak of Jim's *making* those things happen. For granted this way of their coming about, he could have made them happen only by making Pedro shoot . . . it is misleading to think in such a case of Jim having an *effect* on the world through the medium (as it happens) of Pedro's acts; for this is to leave Pedro out of the picture in his essential role of one who has intentions and projects, projects for realizing which Jim's refusal would leave an opportunity.

But if it is misleading to think in such a case of Jim's having an effect on the world through the medium of Pedro's acts, because this leaves Pedro out of the picture in his essential role as someone capable of forming the intention not to shoot, then it is equally misleading to think of Pedro having an effect on the world, for this leaves Jim out of the picture in his essential role as someone capable of assenting to Pedro's proposals and thus (as it happens) preventing Pedro from shooting. Williams's way of setting up the case stipulates the truth of the counterfactual 'If Jim had not refused, Pedro would not have done it', so both Jim and Pedro have an essential role to play. If twenty are to die the 'co-operation' of both men is necessary, and if one is to die their 'co-opera-tion' is necessary; that is the way the example is set up. Of course, what Williams is after is a difference in the causal efficacy of Pedro's and Jim's respective contributions to the deaths of twenty Indians. But this is just what he cannot have; for while Jim cannot make Pedro shoot, Pedro cannot make Jim assent, and if Jim assents, Pedro can no more shoot than he can if (as it might happen) he decides not. For this is Williams's case, and if it is changed so that Pedro is going to shoot whatever Jim does, then it is not of course even causally true that if Jim had not refused Pedro would not have shot.

Making things happen

Williams has put all the weight of his argument on the very tricky notion of making things happen. It is a general feature of negative acts that the agent does not make things happen but rather allows them to occur, but it is far from being a general feature of positive actions that the agent makes things happen, at least in the sense that Williams seems to be relying on. I take this sense to involve some idea of the agent's being in complete control with the capacity to ensure that the event will happen. If I shoot a man intending murder, he may die only if my bullet is not deflected, and moreover hits him in a vital spot, and perhaps only then if the victim does not get to a doctor in time, or if the doctor happens to be ineffi-cient. I cannot make him die, I can only do my best; but if he does die, the fact that in shooting I did not positively *guaran-tee* his demise will not be taken as a mitigating factor. With positive acts it will always be a question of fact whether or not the act does indeed have the expected or probable conse-quences, and the same is true of negative acts. Part of what Williams seems to be relying on in Jim's case is the fact that Jim is powerless and Pedro literally in control. Pedro can make sure that he kills all the Indians if he wants to and Jim can do nothing to stop him but must rely on Pedro's word. But if we change the example so that Jim is in hiding with a machine-gun in the use of which he is an expert, then Pedro cannot make sure of the Indians, he only supposes that he can. For Jim can cut him down even as his finger whitens on the trigger. In this case he is not as might appear the most proximate cause of the deaths of the Indians (if they die) for he needs the acquiescence of Jim, he can only make things happen if Jim lets him. While it is true that Jim cannot make him shoot, nothing Williams says shows that this is a morally or causally relevant fact, any more than it would be morally or causally relevant to say that a doctor cannot *make* a man die of loss of blood by withholding a necessary transfusion.

Olfactory moral philosophy

We must now return to Williams's serious suggestions for dealing with negative responsibility. One of these is the alarming suggestion that a grounded decision 'might not even be decent'.[8]

> Instead of thinking in a rational and systematic way
> either about utilities or about the value of human life,
> the relevance of the people at risk being present and so
> forth, the presence of the people at risk may just have its
> effect. The significance of the immediate should not be
> underestimated . . . very often, we just act, as a possibly
> confused result of the situation in which we are engaged.
> That, I suspect, is very often an exceedingly good thing.

It is interesting to compare Williams's attitude here to Tolstoy's. Talking of Levin towards the end of *Anna Karenina*, Tolstoy remarks:[9]

> Whether he was acting rightly or wrongly he did not know
> — indeed, far from laying down the law, he now avoided
> talking or thinking about it.
>
> Deliberation led to doubts and prevents him from seeing
> what he ought and ought not to do. But when he did not
> think, but just lived, he never ceased to be aware of the
> presence in his soul of an infallible judge who decided
> which of two courses of action was the better and which
> the worse, and instantly let him know if he did what he
> should not.

Williams seems to be recommending here the use of what

Orwell, following Nietzsche, called 'moral nose'.[10] The nose of the basically decent man, being a well adjusted instrument, will tell him what to do, and he will act for the best. But for this sensitive source of moral insmell to operate, it is necessary not only for the immediate to be significant, but for us to be confronted with it, to be, as it were, within sniffing distance. If we are in the presence of the people at risk, their presence might well have its effect and this effect might be for the best. Inasmuch as Williams regards the immediate as a stimulus triggering an automatic response, that is all that can be said, for this response either will, or will not, occur and either will or will not be for the best. But there is also the suggestion that a grounded decision 'might not even be decent'. Consider another recent defender of what we might call the 'olfactory school of moral philosophy'. Noam Chomsky feels that 'by entering into the arena of argument and counter-argument, of technical feasibility and tactics, of footnotes and citations, one has already lost one's humanity.'[11]

But this insistence on the moral priority of the nose is disturbing. For much if not most of what should concern us morally takes place beyond the limited range of our organs of moral sense. If we are to act for the best we must ground not only particular decisions, but the conduct of our lives, on a careful consideration of the many different features Williams points to, seemingly only to reject. 'Out of sight' must not become the justification not only for 'out of mind' but also 'out of account'. Life is no longer easy for the olfactory moral philosopher. 'Civilisation' has been defined as a device for shielding mankind from a cross-section of human experience. The poor are often hidden away in slums, the sick or dying in hospitals, the eccentric or depressed in asylums, the aged are left to die of malnutrition or bronchitis or of cold in the privacy of their own homes, and famine victims live in foreign countries.[12] Moral nose cannot be relied on to prompt us to action on behalf of these people.

The other obvious drawback of moral nose is that we shall want, or we ought to want, to know whether our response to the immediate is the right one; and this we can only find out by trying as best we can in the perhaps limited time available to weigh all the relevant considerations and come to a grounded judgment.

Other people's projects and other people's needs

Another consideration to which Williams attaches great importance, and which he introduces a number of times, is the distinction between my projects and other people's projects. It is from the perspective of other people's projects, as we have seen, that Williams wishes to criticise negative responsibility.[13]

> Discussions of [Jim's case] will have to take seriously the distinction between my killing someone, and its coming about because of what I do that someone else kills them: a distinction based not so much on the distinction between action and inaction, as on the distinction between my projects and someone else's projects.

It is not clear why Williams thinks this a useful distinction. At best it could only touch a small corner of negative responsibility, for the simple and sufficient reason that most of the harm for which we may be negatively responsible is not attributable to the machinations of any people other than those who decline to prevent it. It does not arise from the projects of other people, but rather from such 'natural' causes as disease, famine and drought. The only people involved are those at risk and those who can help them. The weight of Williams's attack on negative responsibility must be borne by the argument from integrity and in this context other people's projects would figure merely as a class of need-creating circumstances, significant only because they highlight the centrality of our own integrity by creating needs which, in crying out to us for help, interfere with our projects.

But in those cases of negative responsibility which do involve other people's projects — and it is significant that both his examples are of this sort — Williams has a special argument. His handling of these two cases suggests that he is really interested in the autonomy and independence of individuals.[14] His point is that if George and Jim do as utility seems to dictate, they would also in effect be surrendering to an alien intelligence, allowing their decisions to be virtually dictated by the projects of another person. This is perhaps why in Jim's case, where his conclusion is that Jim ought to kill one Indian to save nineteen as Pedro suggests, Williams wants Jim to act automatically, to respond directly to the distress of the Indians and not go through the calculations imposed on him by the way Pedro has structured the situation. By following what Tolstoy referred to as 'the infallible judgements of (the) soul', Jim can avoid making any of the calculations Pedro would like to force upon him, he can avoid accepting the range of alternatives that have been imposed by another. In effect he ignores the other person and his projects, and by consulting only his own soul he avoids becoming merely a pawn in another man's game, and remains his own man.

But this shows that the distinction between my projects and other people's projects must be a red herring. Williams wants Jim to come to the same conclusion that he would have come to if he accepted the range of alternatives imposed on the situation by Pedro, but he does not want him to come to the conclusion that way. Jim must act without thinking so that he can both preserve his integrity and come to the right decision. But this sort of attempt to have one's moral cake and eat it is likely to lead to a nasty attack of *mauvaise foi*. Either people must try to convince themselves that they do not know why their actions are right or they are condemned never to wonder whether they have, in fact, done the right thing. Other people's projects must, after all, be seen simply as a class of need-creating circumstances and must, for the purposes of moral decision-making in cases such as George's and Jim's, be treated simply as features of a brutal world, like famine and disease. What I have to choose between is not my projects and other people's projects but my projects and other people's needs. As moral agent I must weigh what they will suffer if I do not help them against what I will suffer if I do. And whether or not in bringing others help I am forced to choose between alternatives imposed on the situation by others cannot make a ha'p'orth of moral difference to me. If I believe that other people are going to carry through their projects with harmful consequences which I can forestall, then for the purposes of moral decision-making I must treat their projects simply as need-creating circumstances. The fact that these people can relent is not relevant if they are not in fact going to relent. The bare fact that it is possible for them to relent can in no way absolve me from the moral duty of weighing the extent of the harm they will cause against the importance of the project I must abandon to forestall the harm.

Blackmail

It may seem that I have made too little of the point that we are here dealing with other agents rather than with brute features of the inanimate world. If I treat them simply as 'need creating circumstances' then I place all the responsibility for the outcome on the bystanders where they refuse to give in to the demands of blackmailers, high-jackers and Pedro.

This is not so, of course. We can and should try to treat agents *as* agents, to reason with them, to remonstrate, to point out the terrible deed they are contemplating and so on. But if all fails, then, come zero hour we must decide. And again, if the best guess is that the Pedros of this world will not relent then I see no alternative to our deciding what to do in the light of what we know will happen if we don't. Again, and again of course, the fact that other agents are involved will affect the issue of blame, but we cannot just pretend that what we decide has no effect on what happens.

Some states, notably Israel, have virtually said to potential high-jackers: 'you must simply treat us as inanimate features of a brutal world because we will not treat with you.' Perhaps part of the idea here is to force terrorists to take responsibility for their actions and certainly public feeling in Israel is usually that the terrorists are solely responsible for what occurs.

These sorts of cases will always be difficult cases but I believe we must think of them as related straightforwardly to other cases of over-determination of events. Where we *assign* blame will depend upon how we feel about the justifications for the actions of all parties in the circumstances. But we should not forget that in such cases there are two ways at least of preventing the disaster and, come zero hour, either the terrorists must relent or the bystanders give in. It may be, as we saw in Chapter 6, that a firm policy of non-capitulation is best calculated to save lives, but this is something bystanders must also bear in mind when deciding what to do.

Conclusion

As a way of criticising negative responsibility Williams's argument from integrity is a non-starter. As we have seen, it applies as much to positive as it does to negative responsibility and in neither case does it cut off our responsibility. Integrity is a factor which might serve to justify our being responsible (positively or negatively) for the harm in question, but it does not help us with moral dilemmas, for the dilemmas, at least the dilemmas Williams considers, are about what price to put on our integrity. Despite disclaimers, Williams talks as though once we realise that our integrity is involved we no longer have to weigh at its full value the cost of persisting in our projects; but he offers no arguments to show why this should be so in any particular case.

His olfactory recommendations are offered without apology as a way of solving and not merely of looking at moral dilemmas. And here we must conclude that far from being 'very often an exceedingly good thing' to solve moral problems nasally, it can never be right to do so. For if Williams were right about olfactory moral philosophy it would be in effect just like the utility machine — simply a piece of apparatus designed to yield instant solutions to complex and agonising moral problems.

Bennett

Jonathan Bennett's[15] principal concern is not with negative responsibility, unlike Williams, but the argument that he deploys to encourage us to be guided more by sympathy than by principles is in the same spirit as that of Williams and, if successful, would give us similar reasons to ignore our principles which dictate that we should avoid harming others and follow the sympathetic dictates of our moral nose.

Jonathan Bennett sets out to explore the consciences of a heterogeneous and fascinating group of characters consisting of Huckleberry Finn, Heinrich Himmler, Jonathan Edwards and Horace, with Wilfred Owen thrown in as a bonus. Bennett's avowed concern is with the relationship between the principles of a bad morality on the one hand and human sympathy on the other. But the interest of his piece lies in the consciences of his characters, and these we are invited to contemplate, I suspect more for their intrinsic interest than for any conclusions we might draw from them either for ourselves or for 'moral philosophy'. The examples are so arresting that they ought to be instructive, but what do we learn from them?

The chief protagonists are Huck Finn and Himmler, and Bennett's examination of the workings of their consciences reveals that even bad moralities may be hard to keep to because those with evil principles may also have sympathies which tempt them to abandon their principles. The central and crucial question then is: how are such dilemmas to be resolved? It is, as Bennett says, dangerous to trust principles because 'it is obviously incoherent for someone to declare the system of moral principles that he *accepts* to be *bad*',[16] so the best course is always to bring our moral principles under 'severe pressure . . . from ordinary human sympathies'.

The trouble is that our sympathies may not be reliable either. Again, as Bennett points out, 'principles, as embodiments of one's best feelings, one's broadest and keenest sympathies . . . can help one across intervals when one's feelings are at less than their best i.e. through periods of misanthropy or meanness or self-centredness or depression or anger.'[17]

Bennett's examination of the relationships between principles and sympathy reveals that since we cannot doubt our principles and therefore cannot be critical of them we'd better rely on our sympathies; while because our sympathies are prone to abate themselves we need principles to see us safely through.

Despite the extreme caution of these findings it is clear that Bennett's sympathies are with sympathy. The whole tenor of his piece quite as much as the fact that he has chosen for his theme the relationship between sympathy and *bad morality* suggests that he shares the view that it is better to rely on feeling than on thought. But whether or not Bennett does want sympathy rather than principles to govern our lives, the relationship between these two, and particularly which we should prefer when facing moral dilemmas, is left as agonisingly unclear at the end of the article as it was at the start.

Perhaps this is because there is something very misleading about the idea of tempering our principles with our sympathy, at least in Bennett's sense of the terms. We should perhaps have been alerted by the oddity of Bennett's explanatory illustration. Before treating us to his virtuoso examples, Bennett explains how principles and sympathy can pull in opposite directions:[18]

> a small child, sick and miserable clings tightly to his
> mother and screams when she tries to pass him over to the
> doctor to be examined. If the mother gave way to her
> sympathy, that is to her feeling for the child's misery and
> fright, she would hold it close and not let the doctor
> come near; but don't we agree that it might be wrong
> for her to act on such feeling? Quite generally, then,
> anyone's moral principles may apply to a particular
> situation in a way which runs contrary to the particular
> thrusts of fellow-feeling that he has in that situation.

At first glance sympathy and principles seem both to pull in the same direction in this example. The mother has fellow feeling (as Bennett puts it) for her child, she does not want it hurt and so should let the doctor treat it, and her principles presumably yield the same conclusion, stating something like: 'help fellow creatures' or more selfishly, 'help fellow creatures for whom you are conventionally responsible'. But since this yields no tug between principles and sympathy it is clear that Bennett has something else in mind.

Natural affection and virtuous principles

There are two conceptions of 'sympathy' at work here. One conception we may think of crudely as the name we give to a sensation or group of sensations which we recognise as occasioned by the plight of other creatures and regard as expressive of concern for them. This sort of sympathy we may or may not feel in appropriate situations. The second conception uses 'sympathy' not so much as the name of a sensation, but rather as the name we give to an attitude to others. In this sense sympathy involves caring about others, it characterises an attitude to others which involves, among many other things, active concern for the welfare of others even when not immediately confronted by their distress and respect for their wishes. This distinction between two conceptions of 'sympathy' mirrors closely that drawn by Bishop Butler[19] between love of our neighbour considered as *natural affection* on the one hand and as a *virtuous principle* on the other, and I shall for convenience adopt Butler's terminology.

The mother and child example seems more to illustrate the conflict between sympathy as a natural affection and sympathy as a virtuous principle, than any tension between sympathy as one sort of thing and moral principles as another. In clutching the child to her bosom the mother's behaviour is expressive of sympathy, but knowing as she does that the child needs the doctor's skills, it could hardly be said to demonstrate concern for the child's welfare.

But now the exhortation 'bring your principles under severe pressure from ordinary human sympathy' which is the normative element of Bennett's piece, can be taken in rather different ways. It can mean: have a moral system which gives sympathy as a virtuous principle a central place and constantly examine your other moral principles, and the application of them, to make sure that they are adequately sensitive to the plight of others; and particularly that they don't leave out of account certain groups of others (Jews and Blacks) for inadequate reasons. This would in effect be the advice to adopt a particular sort of moral system, a set of principles with a particular character. It might perhaps be thought of as the instruction to generalise feelings of natural affection – to be self-conscious about the good of having such feelings, why we value them and what ends they serve.

On the other hand, 'bring your principles under severe pressure from feelings of natural affection' means something like: 'think twice about acting in ways which make you sick'. This is the sense in which Bennett's advice is meant and he values it because he thinks this sort of sympathy universal and regards it as providing a fulcrum which he can use to move moralities in the right direction. The trouble is that without some sense of the value and point of this sort of sympathy, that is without seeing it as part of a general attitude of sympathy, it is just as likely to move moralities in the wrong direction as is obvious from the mother and child example.

So to advise people to give way to natural affection without their having a sense of the point of doing so is bad and dangerous advice, while to encourage them to adopt the virtuous principle of sympathy is just to exhort them to have a good morality or the makings of one. As a fulcrum from which to move the moral universe 'sympathy' is either morally unstable or not a fulcrum.

Finally, it is perhaps worth seeing how Bennett's principal examples of the tension between principles and sympathy fare when looked at from this perspective.

Huckleberry Finn

Huck's dilemma is whether he ought to allow his slave friend Jim to escape to freedom thus cheating Miss Watson of her property or whether he should turn him in. His sympathy for Jim is in conflict with the principles of honesty and gratitude which dictate that he should help to prevent people's property from stealing itself away, especially when he is obliged to the owner. But it is very difficult to ascribe a morality or even any moral principles to Huck. He has some fragments of a morality certainly, a few crude principles relating property rights and a sense of gratitude, but even these are not *his* principles. They are those, as Bennett puts it, 'of rural Missouri' which Huck has taken over quite uncritically and probably unconsciously. Bennett treats moral principles as if it were quite unnecessary that the agent understand or even accept them in the sense of adopting them as his own.[20] Rather they appear as unsolicited imperatives that grab hold of the conscience and drag it willy-nilly in a particular direction. Bennett is treating principles in the way that he treats sympathies, as if they were simply natural affections, brute feelings of what's right which tug the conscience.

The moral we are to draw from Huck's tale is that the best way of solving moral dilemmas is to bring principles (the soundness of which cannot be guaranteed) under severe pressure from sympathies. But this as we have seen is dreadful moral advice, for Huck's sympathies might have been unsound or in abeyance.

To represent Huck as facing a dilemma is really misleading, for Huck does not *decide* to give way to the pressure of his conscience, he just collapses under it. But the question which obviously interests Bennett and which also interests me is how are people who do *face* such dilemmas to resolve them?

Heinrich Himmler

If Huck's problem is that he lacks principles Himmler has the contrary problem — no sympathy; rather he doesn't have sympathy for the right people. Bennett represents Himmler as murdering 'four and a half million (Jews) as well as several million Gentiles' with the utmost regret, stealing himself to do what's right however much against his conscience it may be. But Himmler's sympathies seem not to be so much for his victims as for those Nazis charged with the nasty job of seeing through the final solution. The sympathetic noises Bennett records are Himmler's evincing concern for his own people — not for his victims. Himmler worries lest his men become 'heartless ruffians unable any longer to treasure life'. The problem is to kill Jews 'and to have remained decent fellows'.[21] If Himmler was worried about his victims we might have expected to find some remarks about killing them in the most humane way possible — as if the only barbarity were the gas chambers themselves! Instead we find Himmler saying, again quoted by Bennett, 'what happens to a Russian, to a Czech, does not interest me in the slightest . . . . Whether 10,000 Russian females fall down from exhaustion while digging an antitank ditch interests me only in so far as the antitank ditch for Germany is finished.'[22]

Had Himmler given way to the pressure of his sympathy he would not have spared the Jews or the other non-Aryan victims, he might have tried to get the Japanese to butcher them, or he might have tried to invent even more remotely controlled ways of eliminating them so as to shield his own men from an unpleasant job. Himmler is more like the mother who while by no means a vegetarian or in the slightest interested in humane conditions in abattoirs, does not wish her son to become a butcher because she regards it as a messy, unpleasant and brutalising job and regrets the 'necessity' of her son carrying on the family business. Perhaps all this is just for the record, but I think the collapse of Bennett's chief examples is further evidence that there is something very misleading about the idea of tempering our principles with our sympathy, at least in Bennett's sense of the terms.

No one who treats principles and sympathies as Bennett does is likely to have much success in *resolving* their dilemmas. They are most likely simply to give way under pressure from one or the other, as does Huck. But someone who had some minimum level of self-consciousness about his moral principles, who had some notion of why one might want to be tugged by them or what ends following them are likely to promote or secure, might just be able to bring himself to wonder why no gratitude was owed to Jim or why he was not just as much bound to keep faith with Jim as with Miss Watson. He might even begin to ponder what was at stake for each of them and so see better reasons for keeping faith with one rather than the other. And someone capable of generalising his natural affection for Jim into a virtuous principle would be aware that his sympathy for Jim involved the sense that Jim's welfare and his wishes matter. If Jim's welfare and his wishes really matter to Huck then he can perhaps ask himself whether knowing what Jim will suffer if he turns him in and what Miss Watson will suffer if he doesn't, he would be doing the right thing to turn Jim in.

This is, of course, a naive and crude form of moral argument. But at least a moral argument has got off the ground and I cannot but think that this is a more promising approach to the solution of moral dilemmas than a tug-of-war between an 'unargued natural feeling' and someone else's principles.

Chapter 8

Neutrality

Reporting on Julius Caesar's success in the Civil War Suetonius[1] tells us that 'whereas Pompey declared that all who were not with him were against him and would be treated as public enemies, Caesar announced that all who were not against him were with him.' Jesus was obviously equally impressed with both Pompey and Caesar for he managed to teach both 'he that is not with me is against me'[2] and contrariwise 'he that is not against us is for us'.[3]

In our own times the claim that there can be no such thing as neutrality is as much in vogue as ever it was in the ancient world. Referring to the contemporary denial of neutrality in the context of universities, Leszek Kolakowski[4] remarked in a recent collection of essays on this topic:[5]

The totalitarian conception of the university implies that no human values exist that transcend the particular interests of one or other of conflicting political groups. This principle obviously entails that whatever in the existing spiritual culture cannot be used as a tool for the pursuit of 'our' political goals is necessarily a tool for our 'enemies'.

Caesar, Pompey, Jesus and the totalitarians referred to by Kolakowski are all relying on negative actions to deny neutral status to bystanders. In this chapter we will be examining the question of how far the negative action thesis supports attacks on the possibility of neutrality.

Neutrality and involvement

What is neutrality? Alan Montefiore, in the most extensive recent discussion of the concept of neutrality, defines it thus:[6]

to be neutral in any conflict is to do one's best to help or hinder the various parties concerned in an equal degree.

Kolakowski thinks, on the other hand, that 'I am neutral in relation to a conflict when I purposely behave in such a way so as not to influence its outcome.'[7]

Both Montefiore and Kolakowski make the notion of involvement central to their definitions and both run into difficulties over how to deal with negative involvement.

Identifying neutrality as both an intentional and a causal concept, is to distinguish the elements of thought and deed, and it's worth noting that we can exhibit the intentional aspect of being neutral or impartial without being in a position to help or hinder.

I can support a football team without ever going to watch them play. I am pleased when I hear they've won, vexed when they lose and so forth. It's a pretty hollow form of support but still I am *with* them in a sense. Likewise I may have supported or opposed the American war against the North Vietnamese without having been in a position to influence the outcome. I may be neutral between the parties, both to football matches I cannot influence and to wars I cannot affect. An historian may also be neutral between two or more political factions without any chance of influencing their, now long settled, dispute.

But having noted that there is a purely intentional use for the notion of neutrality it is neutral *behaviour* rather than neutral *attitudes* that most concern both those who defend and those who attack the possibility of neutrality. For the moment then let's try to see where the accounts we are considering go wrong.

First we must remind ourselves that much of the importance of the concept of neutrality lies in its effect on the ascription of responsibility. Here again we see intention appearing as a way of attempting to thwart the ascription of responsibility, as a way of establishing neutrality.

In the epilogue to her study of the Eichmann trial, Hannah

Arendt[8] rejects Eichmann's claim that he was an innocent if not unwitting cog in the Nazi machine and insists that 'politics is not like the nursery; in politics obedience and support are the same thing.'[9] Arendt imagines the judges in Jerusalem rebutting Eichmann's claim that he never acted from base motives and never wanted to kill anyone, nor ever hated the Jews, in the following terms:[10]

> Let us assume for the sake of argument, that it was
> nothing more than misfortune that made you a willing
> instrument in the organisation of mass murder; there still
> remains the fact that you carried out, and therefore
> actively supported, a policy of mass murder.

Now Arendt's concern in attributing *support* of the Nazi mass murders to Eichmann is, despite both Eichmann's and Arendt's disavowals, to show that his mind was with his act. One can almost hear Eichmann telling the court that he was not 'against' the Jews, and Arendt's concern is to rebut this by insisting that in matters of this magnitude (I assume that's what she means by her use of 'politics' in this context) a man must be taken to be in favour of what he does. But this again[11] shows the irrelevance of intention for the ascription of responsibility. What is of moral importance here is that Eichmann knew what he was doing, he set in train the arrangements for mass murders even if he did not himself pull a trigger or close a gas chamber door. What matters is that Eichmann knew what he was doing and did it. One does not make him *more responsible* by deeming him to have 'supported' the policy.

In insisting, eccentrically, that in politics obedience and support are the same thing, Arendt is unnecessarily conceding the importance of intention. She must rely on the fact that Eichmann actually carried out the policy of mass murder, and if he did, the fact that he did or did not support the policy is of relatively minor importance. The issue of *support* would become crucial only if Eichmann had been involved in no other more instrumental way, or if he had claimed that he had acted under duress.

Role playing

Wherever intention appears as a device for limiting responsibility the notion of role playing is sure to be near at hand. Montefiore offers us two examples, one of the referee in a football game whose role it is to be neither with nor against either side in his application of the rules, the other of rather more interest:[12]

> A doctor, whose total personal commitment is to the healing purpose of his profession, may through the force of unwanted circumstances find himself responsible for the care of patients whose fate is of great political importance. There were, for example, German doctors who found themselves in this sort of situation with key Nazi officials as their patients. The doctor may know that if he restores his patient to full normal activity he will return to play a central role in, say, the organisation of concentration camp industries. It would be absurd, so runs the liberal objection, to accuse the doctor of being non-neutral on the side of the Nazis simply because he treated his Nazi patients as any dedicated doctor would treat any patient whatsoever.

Montefiore deals exhaustively with this example. He first notes that there isn't much mileage in trying to decide what the doctor is actually doing, that is whether he is *really* 'treating a patient' or *really* 'restoring a Gestapo leader to full activity'. Neither, he argues, is the question of the doctor's responsibility for his actions, and hence the possible neutrality of his role, much advanced by asking which of the possible action descriptions are descriptions of intentional actions. As we saw in discussion of the difference between killing and letting die,[13] it is always possible that all or none or any intermediate combination of possible action descriptions, are intended by the agent in the sense that he wills, wants, or aims at them. These factors are relevant in the assessment of his character, but not of his responsibility.

What can be made of the 'liberal objection' that the doctor must just treat the sick and by so doing he does not commit himself in any way to the party of any of his patients, nor does he make himself responsible for their actions?

Consider the parallel case of a doctor who falls among thieves, or better still, terrorists. They have forty hostages whom the leader, conveniently suffering from acute appendicitis, has decided to kill. The doctor will be spared on account of his usefulness. There is some dissension in the camp however and the second in command would prefer to release them as a public relations gesture. If the leader dies there's a very good chance the second in command will take over and release them. We'll assume the doctor has the trust of the group and could convince them that the death was an accident and so save himself from any possible recriminations. The hostages are innocent, not politicians, soldiers, nor anyone the terrorists could argue are directly opposed to them or contributing, even negatively, to their plight, whatever it is.

Does the doctor's role allow him either to *remain neutral* in the sense of helping both sides equally, or evade responsibility for the deaths of the hostages, if he does not seize the time and kill the leader? To take the second question first: what can the doctor argue about his role that any ordinary citizen could not also argue? He can say 'my profession is to heal not to injure, to save life not to take it' but who can argue the reverse? (And here we are not interested in 007 agents or soldiers.) None of us are entitled to injure or take life either positively or negatively, and we usually discharge the negative side of this by keeping our clumsy fingers off patients and leaving them to the doctors, except, significantly, where there are no doctors around.

Life saving is everyone's role

No one, not even doctors, can claim they are entitled to kill nor can anyone claim a *special* duty not to. The doctor might claim that the public has a special interest in his discharging his healing role quite impartially, not killing people for political reasons; true, but the public has a special interest in everyone's doing this. No one at all should let people suffer injury because they disagree with them politically or for any other reason except where there are overriding considerations, such as in the present example. The doctor is not a special case in this respect. Finally, if he's interested in preventive medicine, he can save forty lives![14]

Does the doctor's role allow him to remain neutral? He clearly can't evade responsibility because the doctor's role is exceptional even among roles, and we noted earlier[15] the general difficulties about using roles as a means of avoiding responsibility. The doctor in our example is hardly helping the hostages as much as he is the terrorists.

Where palpable help or hindrance is offered to one side more than another the claim that such behaviour is neutral is likely to look pretty thin.

Here we have run up against a quite fundamental difficulty about Montefiore's and Kolakowski's definitions of neutrality. In almost any possible circumstances there will be someone who is entitled to see the would-be neutral as hindering his actions or policies, as influencing the chances of one side or the other. This inevitable dilemma is nicely captured by Montefiore in an example which he abandons without ever working through. His provisional conclusion is that it shows that 'sometimes . . . there is no neutral option available', but he never goes on to give an account of the sometimes when there is. This is the example and I quote it in full because it allows us to draw the conclusions that Montefiore avoids:[16]

> On the other hand the reference to equal (rather than to no) help or hindrance to all the parties concerned runs into certain *prima facie* difficulties of its own. These can best be illustrated in terms of a situation where the parties to the conflict are of evidently unequal strength. To take an example which has no political significance in itself, but which brings out the point very well: two children may each appeal to their father to intervene with his support in some dispute between them. Their father may know that if he simply 'refuses to intervene', the older one, stronger and more resourceful, is bound to come out on top. If he actively intervenes with equal help or hindrance to both of them, the result will necessarily be the same. If he wants to make sure that they both have roughly equal chances of success (that is, if he wants to

render the outcome of their conflict as nearly unpredictable as possible), then he has in practical terms, to help one of them more than the other. In other words the decision to remain neutral, according to the terms of our present definition, would amount to a decision to allow the naturally stronger child to prevail. But this may look like a very odd form of neutrality to the weaker child.

The fact that the parties are of unequal strength does not, of course, make any difference to the possibility of behaving neutrally with respect to them. Whatever the balance of power between the parties, so long as we can have some influence which would favour one or other of them, there will always be someone for whom it will be true that our action or inaction has made him worse off than he would have been had we behaved differently. We can see, at any rate, that we cannot avoid causal involvement in conflicts which we can influence; nor can we hope to help or hinder all parties equally, so that any account of neutrality which depends upon either of these 'possibilities' must fail.

Is there, after all, a sense in which we may be said to be neutral despite our inevitable causal involvement in conflicts to which we are bystanders? Do we have a use for such a sense? Certainly we have an interest in *containing* conflicts: we wish to minimise the number of active participants. The sorts of technical definitions of neutrality which govern international relations and which allow us to say that Switzerland was neutral in the Second World War, depend upon our linking neutrality with non-participation.

Now that we have explored many of the consequences of the negative action thesis, it may seem paradoxical to talk of non-participation when whatever we do influences affairs. How can we be said to be refraining from intervention when we are determining or helping to determine the outcome? How can we decide not to widen a conflict when we are in a sense already involved? It remains true that a conflict which has three active participants is wider in the sense of possessing more parties at risk than a conflict between two participants, even though the two-sided affair includes the bystander in the sense that he exerts a causal influence on the outcome.

How are we to characterise the sense of neutrality relied upon by the technical definitions? If we cannot avoid exercising some causal influence on conflicts, can we characterise neutrality in a way which gives some substance to its claim to be *neutral* or are we after all caught quite literally between the sticks of Pompey or the carrots of Caesar? These are two separate questions and we must keep them distinct. First, is there a viable concept of neutrality? If we cannot help or hinder the parties concerned in equal degree nor can we avoid influencing the outcome, are we thrown back upon the intentional dimension of the concept of neutrality?

Neutrality and treatment as an equal

Ronald Dworkin, in discussing rights, draws a distinction between equal treatment and treatment as an equal. Dworkin is interested in the question of what rights to equality citizens might have:[17]

> There are two different sorts of rights they may be said to
> have. The first is the right to *equal treatment*, which is the
> right to an equal distribution of some opportunity or
> resource or burden . . . . The second is the right to
> *treatment as an equal*, which is the right, not to receive
> the same distribution of some burden or benefit but to be
> treated with the same respect and concern as anyone else.
> If I have two children and one is dying from a disease
> that is making the other uncomfortable, I do not show
> equal concern if I flip a coin to decide which should have
> the remaining dose of a drug. This example shows that
> the right to treatment as an equal is fundamental and
> the right to equal treatment derivative. In some
> circumstances the right to treatment as an equal will
> entail a right to equal treatment but not, by any means, in
> all circumstances.

If we apply the principles Dworkin uses on his children we may see one way out of the problem that faces Montefiore's exemplary children. Montefiore's problem was that, in a dispute between children of different strengths, acting neutrally in his sense 'would amount to a decision to allow the naturally stronger child to prevail. But this may look like a very odd form of neutrality to the weaker child.' It is this odd look that created what Montefiore calls a '*prima facie* difficulty' for his view, although he never shows that it is *only* a *prima facie* difficulty. It's a problem for Montefiore because he feels that the would-be neutral's 'directable causal impacts' on the disputants must be equal. By this insistence on equal treatment Montefiore has given his definition a permanently odd look from the point of view of the presently (or eventually) weaker party.

If we adopt Dworkin's distinction and define neutrality in terms of *treatment as an equal* rather than in terms of *equal treatment* we might be able to avoid the oddity of Montefiore's view. We can say that to be neutral in any conflict is to treat the various parties concerned *as equals*, to treat each with the same concern and respect as that afforded to the others. Now how does this fare as a definition of neutrality? It has high initial promise because we think that a government, for example, should be neutral between its citizens and that it demonstrates this neutrality by showing to each the same concern and respect that it accords to any.

The first thing to note is that this definition is ambiguous between treating the parties to a dispute as equals to *each other* but not necessarily equal to *ourselves*, the would-be neutrals, on the one hand and the requirement that the parties be treated both as equal to each other and to the would-be neutral. The distinction can be important. For example in the case mentioned by Montefiore, of a teacher, say, who takes the knives away from fighting boys and substitutes boxing gloves. So long as one boy was not better with knives and the other with fists we might well regard the teacher as neutral between them, as treating each with the same concern and respect as the other, but he is not treating them as his own equal because he does not allow that they are equally competent to determine their own lives or settle their disputes in their own way. He presumes to mute the harmful effects of their quarrel. This is often the international role of 'neutrals', and since we value their function of limiting the scope of disasters, we have a reason for preserving this unequal dimension of treatment as equals.

There is a further ambiguity over the question of who precisely is to be treated with equal concern and respect to whom. The case of the doctor who fell among terrorists and who was faced with a decision as to whether to treat the terrorist leader and 'condemn' forty hostages to death or kill the terrorist with the almost certain consequence that the hostages will be released, presents a problem: how do we advise the doctor to act if he wishes to be *neutral*? If every man is to count for one and none for more than one, then the doctor will hardly be treating the parties as equals if he saves the terrorist. But if we use the Benthamite calculus we must advise neutrals always to support the more numerous side! Alternatively, we might decide to treat identifiable factions as the entities to whom treatment as an equal is owed. Here a number of plausible interpretations might be given to the instruction to treat the parties with equal concern and respect. We cannot investigate them all here but it is worth noting that one of the most obvious interpretations, indeed the one illustrated by Dworkin (although he is not illustrating a concept of neutrality), yields highly partisan results. For imagine that we, our nation, are bystanders to a conflict involving a large power that wishes to annexe a smaller one, how should we behave if we wish to be neutral? On the present view we should take into account what each has to lose and, as with Dworkin's children, aid the one whose very existence is threatened. But a concept of neutrality which required us always to aid the weaker party would prove unacceptable to all but weaker parties. It could hardly be adopted as a rule to be observed by all neutrals in international conflicts.

Most of the various interpretations that might be given to the instruction to treat the parties to any conflict with equal concern and respect involve going into the merits of the rival cases. As in the above example where we have to weigh what each party stands to lose, or where we have to protect the weak, or, as in competition for jobs or other opportunities, invoke policies of compensatory discrimination.

Neutrality as treatment as an equal would give us a concept of neutrality which abandoned the non-participation requirement (indeed it would make *participation a requirement* in most cases), but it would leave us with a course of action, or a number of such courses, which are intelligibly neutral. Intelligibly neutral because some conception of equality in our treatment of the parties does seem to be fundamentally involved in our thinking of any behaviour as 'neutral'.[18] Perhaps this is the concept of neutrality we ought to have, but I fear that it will hardly recommend itself to the members of the United Nations Security Council. Let's try a slightly different tack.

Neutrality and the avoidance of preference

Once we have delved into the rival merits of conflicting parties we are very unlikely to be able to treat them in any way which would recommend itself to anyone as *neutral* in the sense of equality of treatment. But suppose that when we investigated the merits of each of the conflicting parties we were equally impressed by all. Suppose that, all in all, we could find nothing to choose between them; each party seemed to us to have an equally valid claim on our aid. What then should we do? I think we would refrain from interfering, that we would keep out of the conflict, for we have no reason to *prefer* the victory of one over another. We would, in short, be neutral between them. So what if we recommend anyone who wishes to be neutral to behave as if he had gone into the merits of the rival cases meticulously and could find *absolutely nothing to choose between them*? What would such a person do? A man who sees no possible reason for helping one rather than another will, we have supposed, refrain from intervening. To be sure, this will amount to a decision to allow the stronger party to prevail, and in this sense the man who stands by as a neutral will be having a 'directable causal impact' on the dispute which favours one or another, he will necessarily be influencing the outcome. But since, *ex hypothesi* he has no reason to prefer the victory of one rather than another, he has no reason to re-arrange the victory awarded by fate. Of course he almost always will have such a reason, and that will be a reason to abandon his neutrality, it will be a reason *not* to act as if he could find nothing to choose between them, it will be a reason to *prefer* one of the parties.

It is important to note just how the avoidance of preference, which involves the presumption of equal merit, differs from treatment as an equal. A person who has gone into the merits of rival cases and can find nothing to choose between them will not, I suggest, act as he would if he believed that each was equally entitled to the *same* concern and respect, but as if each was entitled to *all* his concern and respect (the only trouble is he cannot decide which). To put this point another way: the person who wishes to treat the rivals as equals may act so as to put them on an equal footing and this may involve, for example, compensatory discrimination. Whereas the 'neutral' who refuses to prefer one party to another will act as though each party to the conflict is equally justified, will act as if he believed that each was entitled to complete victory. And since he cannot find a reason to support one rather than the other, he will stay out of the conflict altogether, for he can change, only gratuitously, the determination of fate. If he tossed a coin, for example, and then helped the winner, he would simply be subjecting the outcome to fate twice over (and to no purpose). If, however, *both* parties were about to perish and he could save only one, the neutral would properly toss a coin to see which to rescue, for now he has a reason. Although he doesn't prefer to save one rather than another it is (presumably) better that one should survive than none.

It has not been my intention to argue in any conclusive way for either neutrality as *treatment as an equal* or as the *presumption of equal merit*. These alternative accounts are offered as suggestions of possible ways of defining neutrality which do not involve the impossible task of avoiding causal involvement in disputes.

The merit of these ways of thinking about neutrality is that they make clear a fact that other conceptions conceal or deny. Namely, that it is impossible to have clean hands in any dispute that one can influence, and uninteresting to claim neutrality where one cannot but be entirely ineffectual.

We are left with either the honestly involved conception of neutrality as treating the parties as equals, and the honestly fictitious presumption of equal merit.

Chapter 9

The bounds of obligation

Innocence is easily lost, but no innocence is lost so easily as the innocence of innocent bystanders. Is the causal and moral symmetry of positive and negative actions the forbidden fruit that banishes innocence forever from the garden of action? Less fancifully, is there any way of keeping from our hands the blood of those we might have helped and, rather less importantly, of justifying ourselves before their friends?

Belief in the possibility of a genuinely neutral neutrality or in the virtues of non-intervention or non-participation tends to be eroded by acceptance of the negative actions thesis. And as the possibility of avoiding exercising an influence on events which we can effect recedes, so our sense of the consequent boundlessness of our obligation to exercise that influence for the best increases. We must now see whether this apparent boundlessness is real, and if it is, whether it is really objectionable.

To answer these questions we must first look at the degrees of effectiveness with which bystanders are able to intervene and consider what difference, if any, the number of bystanders makes. We will then examine a very abstract argument that might be levelled at the negative actions thesis and which attacks it precisely because of the apparent boundlessness of the obligations it imposes on us all. Finally, we will assess some general consequences of the boundlessness of our negative responsibility.

The effectiveness of intervention

Clearly, in determining the status of the bystanders we want to know whether they are (or were) in a position to intervene and what sort of intervention was open to them. Let's first note some of the possibilities.

1 Decisive intervention
As we have seen, where a person can intervene decisively he will be causally responsible for the outcome whatever he does. Where, however, he can intervene decisively only in combination with others the situation is complicated in a number of ways:

a)   He is a necessary part of the combination.
b)   He is not.
c)   The others are going to intervene anyway.
d)   They will intervene only if they can do so effectively, i.e. with him or others or on some other contingency.
e)   They must be persuaded.
f)   Those necessary for decisive intervention won't act.

2 Significant intervention
Here the individual cannot intervene decisively, he cannot secure an outcome either alone or in combination with others, but he can make a significant contribution, he can give one side a better chance. And again, if the individual's contribution will only be significant as part of a concerted effort, then the situation will be complicated by the above sorts of alternative.

3 Inconclusive intervention
In very many cases, while it is true that someone could influence events and also true that his non-intervention has a causal impact, it is not clear either:

a)   how the individual can influence events to any particular end;
b)   what effect any attempted influence will have;
c)   in cases of conflict between persons or parties which side either intervention or failure to intervene would help.

Many examples spring to mind, but a quarrel between husband and wife or a dispute between neighbours over a boundary fence would be familiar examples. A case of more global import would be whether Switzerland's neutrality in the Second World War helped the Allies or the Axis?

4   Token intervention

Here it is envisaged that there is little or no chance of the individual's intervention (either alone or in combination) swinging the result or even making much of a difference. What he can do is 'stand up and be counted'.

5   Emphatic denunciation

Rather like token intervention except that here it is too late to intervene even in a token way. It is still possible, however, to show what one thinks, to make an unequivocal moral gesture.

The status of the bystander, the nature of his involvement, the degree of his responsibility, will obviously depend on the sort of impact he might, or might have, made on affairs, and the nature and importance of the struggle or event by which he is standing. The different features will of course be weighted differently by different people and this will make the status of the bystanders a contestable and often contested issue. But those who could at best be *with* Jesus, for example, in only a token sense are hardly responsible for his death and are not in any event as closely involved as, say, Pilate, whatever Jesus might say to the contrary.

   Whether or not we say with Caesar that those who are not against us are with us, or with Pompey that those who are not with us are against us, is largely a matter of stance or of *realpolitik*. With a war to win and recruits to encourage or possible enemies to neutralise,[1] it is a matter of personality whether rival generals settle for the stick of Pompey or the carrot of Caesar. The awful question lurking here is whether or not the Caesars and Pompeys of this world are entitled to set about us with sticks and carrots dragging us into their private or public, intimate or global conflicts? Are governments entitled to say, as a number have done in recent times, that those who are not with us are against us? Indeed, it might be asked, isn't it just the sort of negative responsibility thesis here advanced, that has lead Russia, for example, to adopt the Pompey doctrine?

The answer is, I think, that we can be held responsible for what we are responsible for. But this does not give *carte blanche* to the Pompey doctrine. Whether we think governments entitled to act on the view that if we are not with them we are against them, and here this must mean 'treat us as an enemy', will depend on what view we take about the desirability of opposition as part of our theory of government (in some countries 'being against' is constitutive of the system). Whether or not a Pompey or a Caesar or indeed a more modern terrorist is *entitled* to treat us as an enemy will depend again on the degree of our responsibility. The terms 'enemy' and 'with' and 'against' as we have been rather freely using them here are not very helpful.

If we are dealing, say, with a terrorist group fighting 'for' the Palestinian Arabs then the sense in which we, the airline passengers caught in a high-jack, are 'against' the terrorists will depend on our responsibility for the plight of the Palestinians. That is, on the sort of help we might have given: decisive, significant, merely token and so on. Whether or not we *ought* to have given what help we could, whether or not we are justified in being responsible for their plight to whatever degree we are, and whether their plight is such as to warrant killing to ameliorate it, are other questions and ones I assume the terrorists have already decided to their satisfaction.

I see no way out of our having to assess in each case the responsibility of bystanders for the events they might have influenced. Although enormously difficult this is, I think, preferable to relying on often spurious and hypocritical distinctions between killing and letting die or between combatants and non-combatants, neutrals and belligerents.

Minding one's own business

It would undoubtedly be a disadvantage if the theory of negative actions turned out to be, in effect, a busybody's charter. If we are in a position to influence events, are we obliged always to do so for the best? Should we always intervene in disputes to help the party we judge to be in the right? These are separate questions.

1 Occam's Razor

Where we are capable only of inconclusive intervention, where it is unclear what effect our intervention will have, where our intervention is unlikely to aid the side we wish to aid, or unlikely to shorten the dispute, or unlikely to ameliorate the situation, and where there are no special reasons for *token intervention* or *emphatic denunciation*, then we will have a reason for declining to intervene. This reason would be a sort of principle of economy or Occam's Razor, which would cut off unnecessary entities or simplify disputes, by preferring those with fewer active members.

2 Other people's business

There are a large number of cases where we recognise that we are, or recognise that we are regarded as being, outside the context of the parties engaged in the dispute. We or they regard the affair as being none of our business. We are not members of the family, the club, the organisation or the community; there is no interest of ours at stake, we are not committed to the issues involved and so on. Whether or not we should intervene in such cases will depend, very much as it has always done, on what is at stake. It would be pointless to try and be more precise here. We may recognise that our neighbours' methods of rearing their children are not of the best, but also recognise that it is genuinely none of our business. We might well, by careful and patient interference, improve things somewhat, but it is a marginal issue, and the expected results do not merit the effort required or the bad feeling that might result. It might even advance utility if we interfered, but not perhaps to any great extent. To be sure, we are responsible for not improving the lot of the children by even as much as we might have done, but we would rather be responsible for this than for interfering in the lives of our neighbours. But if, on the other hand, the children are suffering severe neglect or cruelty we will undoubtedly feel differently about the merits of minding our own business.

The disappearance of an option of non-involvement does not lead inevitably to the totalitarianism advocated by Pompey and Jesus and feared by Kolakowski. It may entail that 'whatever in the existing spiritual culture cannot be used as a tool of our political goals is necessarily a tool for our enemies', but it does not force anyone to adopt political goals which preclude impartial enquiry or demand intolerance of the views even of enemies. Nor does it entail that a Pompeian rather than a Caesarian attitude be adopted. What it does involve, however, is a morality which enjoins the scrutiny both of our actions and of our opportunities to act and which makes us face up to the consequences of the ways in which we influence the world.

Is the kind of scrutiny we give to these questions affected by the numbers of bystanders there are or by the fact that some of these may be collectives of various kinds: commercial companies, universities, government agencies and nation states?

More than one bystander

Let's consider two cases. The first is one in which we are immediately confronted with an opportunity to save a life and where others known to us are similarly placed and we can see what they will do. The other, more remote, in which we can save some lives but we do not know how many, and where others are similarly placed, but we neither know who they are nor what they will do.

Case 1
A man is drowning. On the beach a hundred expert swimmers, including ourselves equally accomplished, can see that he will drown unless he is rescued. If no one makes any attempt to save the swimmer then each can see that, given the inertia of

the others, it is true that but for his own inactivity, the swimmer would not have become a sinker.[2]

We must remember that each of the thousand bystanders was an accomplished swimmer, each, we are to suppose, could have achieved a rescue without danger to himself, with, it's true, a certain amount of exertion but which, one would think, would be more than adequately compensated for by the satisfaction of having saved a life, the gratitude of the victim and the esteem of his fellow men. Of course it is true, or at least we will assume that it is true, that none of the thousand intended or desired the death of the drowned man, that they had no interest in his death and that it was of no use to them.

The circumstances of this case offer no excusing conditions, the accomplished swimmers would not have had to risk their own lives to save the drowning man. All these swimmers are in the same boat as regards their causal responsibility for the death of the drowned man. I can see no reason why the swimmers should not be in the same moral boat also. What should save them from liability responsibility for the death of the drowned man? Surely not the accident that there were rather a lot of people involved.

We must enter one *caveat*. If one rescuer goes to the aid of the drowning swimmer then the other nine-hundred-and-ninety-nine may consider the obligation discharged, unless, of course it is obvious that one rescuer is not enough. If the would-be rescuer fails for one reason or another and there is no time or opportunity for any subsequent rescue attempts, we would not, I think, blame any of the other bystanders even though it might be true of each of them that had he gone as well, the swimmer would not have been drowned. The point is a practical one and obvious enough. So long as we know that help is on the way to the victims of whatever the disaster, and have no reason to suppose that the help will not prove equal to the task in hand, then we have a right to assume that the victims, if not no longer at risk, are being given the best chance of surviving. To fail to make this assumption would be a wanton squandering of resources.

Case 2

Most of us could afford to give a certain amount of money which we do not at present give and which we can be certain would be enough to save at least one victim from starvation in Asia or Africa. We don't know who will be saved if we give this figure, nor do we know what (most) other people are doing. We do, however, know that some people will die for want of the aid that we could give.[3]

Are we responsible for the plight of what is now called the 'Third World'? Do we, in the so-called advanced countries of the world, stand to the people of the Third World as, for example, the English society of the 1840s stood to the English working class?

First, we must settle who 'we' are. We have seen that the presence of more than one bystander cannot make any difference to the responsibility of any of them (with the exception already noted). This will be true even if the other bystanders include large corporations or even nations (and these collectives of course include us). We will, therefore, continue to concentrate on the responsibility of the individual although he may, as we shall see, discharge the responsibility with the collective in mind.

There seems to be two principal alternatives: an individual might feel that he must simply give as much as he can to enable the Third World to buy or produce more food or medical supplies or whatever else is needed. Struck by the vastness of their need and the comparative insignificance of any individual contribution, he might on the other hand feel that he must try to mobilise mass aid or perhaps attempt to persuade his government to provide the massive aid that only state apparatus can give. Let us explore the first alternative.

Individual responsibility

If the individual elects to give as much as he can, does he in this way avoid responsibility for death in the Third World? Here there is a difficulty, for there seems to be no cut-off point. If we suppose that one pound will save one life, it is not difficult to see that we ought to give one pound, since most people in England can afford to part with that much at least: and if one pound will prevent a death then to withhold one pound is to let someone die. But one pound more will save another life, and since the loss of two pounds would put few of us into bankruptcy, we must clearly give the second one pound as well, if we are not to be responsible for the death which giving it will prevent. Every obligation to save a life which we discharge reveals another behind it. Every time we pay our debt, we owe it again, and so on until we are ourselves bankrupt. There can be no turning back, since the lives of human beings are at stake. This is clearly going further than most people would be prepared to go. But perhaps this is the only way to avoid responsibility for the deaths of others.

If we really are bystanders to the plight of those dying of hunger or malnutrition, the fact that our obligation to prevent death has no cut-off point cannot mean that there is, after all, no obligation. We must just go on until our capacity to help is exhausted — as we would have to do if hundreds of children were drowning before our eyes and we competent swimmers. In such a case we would have to go on bringing them ashore until we were so exhausted that there was a very real possibility that we would ourselves be drowned if we attempted another rescue. We could not just stop at some arbitrary point and say 'that's enough for today!'. But do we, *vis-à-vis* our individual resources, stand to those in the Third World as we do to the children drowning before our eyes?

Certainly we don't, or most of us don't, feel the same way about it. What happens on 'the other side of the world' is something to deplore, but not something that we can, or perhaps even should, do very much about. Of course distance has a distancing effect, but although remoteness is, as we have seen, often cited as the reason for our relative indifference, it is not the sort of thing that could get us off the moral hook. The Third World may be 'thousands of miles away', but it is only a few hours' flying time. If there is something we genuinely *can* do to prevent death and starvation, then if we are not to be responsible for those deaths we must prevent them. Do we indeed stand to the people of the Third World as we do to those dying before our eyes? What possible difference could remoteness make unless it affects the possibility or the effectiveness of aid, which in this case it clearly does not?

For the individual the task of doing all he can to prevent preventable deaths in the Third World is genuinely unremitting. The individual would literally have to work and give tirelessly, every one pound given would reveal another one pound 'owed', every minute's rest would cost lives, every hour's recreation would be bought with the suffering of others. To save the drowning children we might have to work ourselves to the point of exhaustion for an hour or so but then we could rest. To save all the lives that we can in the Third World is an endless task requiring literally remorseless effort.

It seems to be the inescapable conclusion of our argument so far (given the premise that we accept a principle that we ought not to bring harm to others if we can help it) that a person ought to go on giving to or working for others until he is as badly off as those he is trying to help.

But there is perhaps a general if abstract argument against this conclusion. We must see now whether we can be rescued from our exhausting task by the effect that the prospect of such a task has on our own, or on our society's, moral consciousness.

The second order argument

This is an argument against the boundlessness of negative responsibility and for the demolition of the moral distinction between positive and negative infliction of harm, between killing and letting die. I will call it 'the second order argument'. If it is true, so the argument might go, that our negative responsibilities have this boundless character, then our knowledge that we cannot hope to discharge them fully will weaken our resolve to discharge them at all. Moreover, if we become convinced that the harm which results from negative actions is every bit as bad as the harm which results from positive actions, our resolve not to do positive harm will weaken with our resolve not to do negative harm. And because we cannot feel guilt at all the negative harm we cause, we will gradually cease to feel guilt at any of it, and consequently cease to feel guilt when we inflict harm positively. The result will be a general erosion of our moral values and a much worse sort of society.

It is better, according to this argument, to have a simple and not too demanding morality which we can hope to keep to and which we will feel guilty about breaching, than a much more demanding morality which we must cease to respect because we cannot hope to observe its massive demands. The second order argument might also wish to claim that the strict prohibitions against harming others by positive actions work so well that it is dangerous to undermine confidence in them by demolishing the moral difference between positive harm and mere failures to aid.

Two things must immediately strike us about this sort of argument. The first is that it is naive to suppose that a morality which maintains the moral difference thesis is doing so well for us. The sorts of continual disasters which it permits and which we have reviewed in the preceding chapters must put paid to this sort of justification.

The second point is that it is an act of faith that the acceptance of negative responsibility will have the sort of effect on morality that is envisaged. Christian morality, for example, has long made its adherents painfully conscious of the fact that they are all sinners, without supposing that this feature in particular has undermined their confidence in the morality of which this feeling is a consequence. It is, after all, a characteristic of most moralities worthy of the name that they take some living up to.

Just how large a leap of faith is required to believe that the demolition of the moral difference between positive and negative actions will result in the collapse of morality is likely to be a contested issue, so it is worth exploring a little further the various ways in which the second order argument might be put.

A second order moral difference

A proponent of one form of the second order argument might reason as follows:

You say that the distinction between positive and negative ways of inflicting harm, between acts and omissions, is a distinction without a moral difference and that we should therefore revise our moral rules accordingly. But it is probable that demolition of this distinction would have a bad effect on our willingness to keep to our moral principles (for reasons already rehearsed) and *this* constitutes a moral difference between positive and negative actions.

We must remind the proponent of this version of the second order argument that the negative actions thesis denies that there is a moral difference between positive and negative actions with the *same consequences*. This version of the second order argument does not show that there is, after all, a moral difference between positive and negative actions with the *same* consequences, but that the acceptance of the belief that there is no such difference will *itself* make a difference to the total consequences of our actions. If this type of second order argument is right, harmful positive actions are worse, more to be avoided, than harmful negative actions with the same apparent consequences, because, if harmful positive actions are not shunned more than their negative counterparts, this will have remote effects which will alter the total consequences.

This argument, though ingenious, has a number of defects. At best it could show, not that there is a moral difference between positive and negative actions with the same consequences, but rather that it will never be true in practice that positive and negative actions do have the same consequences. However, in many cases it will simply not be true that acting on the belief that there is no moral difference between positive and negative actions with the same apparent consequences will feed back into our own, or our society's, moral consciousness so as to change significantly, or at all, the total consequences of the acts in question. It will not, therefore, be the case that positive actions are inevitably or intrinsically more harmful than negative actions with the same apparent consequences because of the feedback effect.

In other cases the degree of harm involved in resolutely refusing to harm anyone positively when we can thereby save the lives of very many others, will be such as to make it grotesque to refuse to do so because our willingness to act similarly at some future time might thereby be undermined.

Two-tier morality

There is a way of deploying the second order argument which locates the moral difference not in a contrast between the consequences of positive and negative actions, but in the moral psychology of contrasting societies, where one society makes a moral distinction between positive and negative actions and the other does not. The argument then is that a society which draws a moral distinction between positive and negative actions is a society capable of internalising its morality. In such a society people can feel acute guilt, shame and remorse because they only need do so when they kill or injure positively. If they had to feel the same about killing or injuring negatively they would have to feel acute guilt, shame and remorse all the time. This would either prove impossible, or relegate these emotions to the position of having a general souring effect on our lives rather than playing their part in regulating and reinforcing our morality. In short, a society which allowed these emotions their proper place would inevitably be a more morally aware society and one in which our distressing moral emotions kept us up to the mark. In the alternative society our willingness to avoid the infliction of harm would wither as our guilt evaporated, with obvious and catastrophic results.

Here again I think it implausible to believe that our guilt-ridden society has done so well for us in the past. This is not the place to review again the very many examples of the disasters that arise from accepting a moral difference thesis, but they comprise a formidable indictment of any morality embodying this thesis. Of course the second order argument does not commit its defenders to the view that one need feel *no* guilt at the harm caused by negative actions, only that the guilt cannot be of nearly the same order of magnitude. But again it would have to be far clearer than it is from any available evidence that the consequences of abandoning the moral difference thesis would be so cataclysmic as to warrant our clinging to the view that killing one man positively is so much worse than killing very many negatively. Yet another version of the second order argument was put forward recently by R.M. Hare.[4] Hare starts by distinguishing two levels of moral thinking:[5]

The first (level 1) consists in the application of learned principles, which, in order to be learned have to be *fairly* general and simple; the second (level 2) consists in the criticism, and possibly the modification, of these general principles in the light of their effect in particular cases, actual and imagined. The purpose of this second, reflective kind of thinking is to select those general principles for use in the first kind of thinking which will lead to the nearest approximation, if generally accepted and inculcated, to the results that would be achieved if we had the time and the information and the freedom from self-deception to make possible the practice of level-2 thinking in every single case. The intuitions which many moral philosophers regard as the final court of appeal are the result of their upbringing − i.e. of the fact that just these level-1 principles were accepted by those who most influenced them.

Hare concedes that 'we shall not obtain any morally relevant difference between acts and omissions, provided that we are engaged in level-2 thinking', but goes on to make the following argument for re-introducing the moral difference at level-1:[6]

However it may well be that the level-1 principles, which we selected as a result of this (level-2) thinking, *would* use the distinction between acts and omissions. The reason for this is that, although this distinction is philosophically very puzzling and even suspect, it is operable by the ordinary man at the common sense level; moreover it serves to separate from each other classes of cases which a more refined thinking would also separate . . . . Thus

there may be no morally relevant distinction . . . between
killing and failing to keep alive in *otherwise identical
cases*; but if people have ingrained in them the principle
that it is wrong to kill innocent adults, but not always
wrong to fail to keep them alive, they are more likely
in practice to do the right thing than if their ingrained
principles made no such distinction. This is because most
cases of killing differ from most cases of failing to keep
alive in *other* crucial ways, such that the former are very
much more likely to be wrong than the latter.

The obvious recommendation here is surely that more, and
more careful, thinking at level-2 should be able to produce
level-1 principles which captured these '*other* crucial' differences and did not preserve a 'highly suspect' distinction. I am
not as pessimistic as Hare about the common man's ability to
do, or follow, level-2 thinking and it is better to encourage
people to do this sort of thinking, in short to encourage them
to become moral agents, than for them slavishly to adhere to
suspect principles.

One principle that careful level-2 thinking yields is: Do not
harm others if you can possibly avoid doing so, and if you
cannot avoid harming others then do as little harm as possible.
And this principle demands that we abandon the moral
difference thesis.

Some philosophers have assumed that the consequential
boundlessness of our obligations is in itself a *reductio ad
absurdum* of negative responsibility. Bernard Williams[7] takes
this for granted:[8]

Again this issue of negative responsibility can be pressed
on the question of how limits are to be placed on one's
apparently boundless obligation implied by utilitarianism,
to improve the world. Some answers are needed to that
too – and answers which stop short of relapsing into the
bad faith of supposing that one's responsibilities could
be adequately characterised by appeal to one's roles.

Williams seems to assume that negative responsibility theorists
are in big trouble unless they can find a way to limit the
apparently boundless obligation to prevent harm, although he
does accept the inadequacy of the 'roles solution' to this

problem criticised in Chapter 3. But is this 'boundless obligation' *eo ipso* objectionable?

Original sin

For one thing it gives substance to the insight into the human condition expressed by at least one version of the doctrine of original sin. If we think of 'sin' as 'the avoidable infliction of harm on other people', then it looks as though sin in this sense is truly inevitable; we cannot help being sinners. This looks as though it involves a contradiction, because if we cannot help inflicting suffering then it is not avoidable and therefore no sin. But this contradiction is apparent rather than real. For even if someone spent every available minute of his life working for the needy, who could say that another minute might not have been found, a minute's less rest here or there which might have been used to save another life? The limits of what it is possible for anyone to do to prevent harm to others are always such as to admit the possibility of extension. It looks very much as though, however paradoxical it may sound, we cannot, for all practical purposes, avoid inflicting suffering on our fellows and that we are all sinners in this sense.

Of course while we may all be sinners it does still very much matter how great sinners we are. The apparent boundlessness of our obligations cannot mean that we do not in fact have these obligations any more than the boundlessness of disease is an argument against the practice of medicine. It is perhaps not so discouraging if we remember that the overwhelming nature of the task would be mitigated dramatically if contemporary morality changed for the better. It would then look neither so hopeless nor so boundless a prospect. If it were shared and respected by all, the obligation not to harm our fellows would be far from boundless for each.

Thought and action

One further uncomfortable consequence of the boundlessness of the task which the negative actions thesis imposes on us, is the inevitable gulf between our beliefs and our intention to act on them. If we believe that we should not inflict harm on our fellows if we can help it, then we must believe that we ought to go on preventing harm to our fellows as long as we can. But we have no intention of doing so, it's too difficult.

Now as with the boundlessness of our obligation so here, many philosophers would believe that this admission is a knock-down argument against the thesis here presented. Characteristically they would say 'I ought entails I shall' and 'I ought but I shall not is a contradiction'.[9] This view has a long and august tradition stretching back to Socrates[10] and is at its most plausible when we ask how we are to judge a person's sincerity. If the body is the best picture of the human soul, a man's actions are the best evidence for his beliefs. If a man says that he believes he ought to do something and when the time comes he doesn't do it, nor does he exhibit regret or remorse, we will be inclined to conclude that he didn't really believe in what he said.

This moral behaviourism, while not quite as disreputable as its psychological counterpart, nonetheless enjoys rather more currency than it deserves. As in other areas, the best test of a person's beliefs is sincere avowals and the tests of sincerity are many and various, only one of which is correspondence with actions. The demolition of moral behaviourism is a large task and one quite outside our present concerns. I shall have to be content with a couple of points. We are all familiar with the man who knows he ought to give up smoking or rich food or both because they are killing him, and who knows that he never will. He is sincere but . . . in many cases the trouble is that he acquired his beliefs too late to change his habits. It is a bit like this with us.

And if to save *our own* lives we cannot find the resolution to give up smoking or rich food, how much more 'impossible' will seem the task of changing our way of life, or our priorities, to help others.

But things which seem remote when first mooted can

move rapidly from the fantastic to the commonplace. Ideas, particularly moral ideas, which look utopian or ridiculous to one generation, are the basic morality of its successors. As and when acceptance of the importance of negative actions gains ground, the morality that their acceptance indicates will become more realistic.

Meanwhile I think we can sincerely hold that we ought to prevent literally all the harm that we can *and* recognise that we are not going to find the saintliness to do anywhere near as much as we believe that we should. Unlike the man above we probably will show our regret and even remorse that we will not find the courage of our convictions. This is not a happy position to be in, but it is I think both philosophically and morally preferable to the bad faith involved in seeking ways to show that there is nothing wrong in our failing to prevent harm that we could prevent.

Collective responsibility

Faced with problems as vast as the plight of all the needy people in the world, the individual may well feel paralysed. Whatever one might do is just a drop in the ocean; a drop that while not lost in reality is invariably lost in the imagination. The alternative to contributing on an individual basis is to attempt to mobilise mass or government or institutional aid for the needy.

This might take a number of forms. Fund raising is the most obvious but it is also possible to bring various forms of pressure to bear upon governments or other institutions, who may themselves be other bystanders to the fate of those in need, better able both to help and to absorb the sacrifice of so doing. This seems a more promising way of seeing that everyone has enough to eat, and considering the number of lives that could thereby be saved, it does seem to be something that we are clearly obliged to do. We are obliged to mobilise these corporations and they are obliged to act; at least if they subscribe to the principle that they ought not to cause death or suffering if they can avoid doing so. And if they do act on the vast scale of which they are capable, there is no doubt that at least so far as money and expertise are of use, they can render the vast individual sacrifices we have been considering unnecessary. It is possible but by no means certain, that a lowering of the general standard of living of the people of the rich countries and a re-think about what is to count as legitimate expenditure will be necessary; but certainly not a general reduction to the level of penury we have been considering.

But what if, as at present, adequate corporate aid is not forthcoming? The individual who tries to mobilise such aid in the vast and impersonal modern 'democracies' has little expectation of success. The task is as great as that of trying to save the world single-handed and just as potentially exhausting. Knowing in advance how futile the supposed 'avenues of influence' on government are for the ordinary citizen, it is difficult to feel that by making routine walks down them we are fulfilling our obligation to the starving.

And if we go further and try somehow to force governments to give the massive aid they are capable of and which would most effectively supply the needs of the needy, we know our chances of success are small. We know the same will be true of the individual's attempts to divert resources from those things for want of which people will not die, to those for want of which they will.

The result of facing these facts is likely to be cynicism, the cynicism so brilliantly diagnosed by Bertrand Russell when he noted that it arose from a combination of comfort with powerlessness. 'Powerlessness', he said, 'makes us feel that nothing is worth doing and comfort makes the painfulness of this feeling just endurable.'[11]

To recognise this is to feel the tremendous pressure against radical change that exists in societies like our own where 'there is only one argument for doing something; the rest are arguments for doing nothing'.[12] The negative actions thesis underpins one argument for doing something. By showing us how much of the suffering in the world is brought about by our negative actions, it shows us that if we do not wish to harm others, we must organise our lives and our societies to minimise the negative infliction of harm.

To say this is, of course, to leave all the most difficult

tasks undone. To change ourselves and the world so that we cause the least possible harm will involve the resolution of incompatibly strong claims on scarce resources and agonising choices between evils. The bringing about of this change will undoubtedly be a very long process, but a necessary prelude to this change must be an understanding of just what we are doing to one another.

I believe that the negative actions thesis helps in achieving such an understanding. It widens the horizon of our actions and consequently of our responsibilities. This horizon like any other, will recede as we approach it, but this fact cannot prevent progress towards it from being worthwhile, nor can it render futile the preliminary work of clearing the ground.

Notes

Chapter 1 Humans and persons

1 A thousand has been mentioned in this connection.
2 See Ludgwig Wittgenstein, *Philosophical Investigations* (Oxford, 1963), S. 342.
3 See R. Allen and Beatrice Gardner, 'Teaching Sign Language to Chimpanzees', *Science*, vol. 165, 1969, pp. 664-72, and Eugene Linden, *Apes, Men and Language*, Harmondsworth, 1975.
4 So great indeed that its powers are compatible with most people's conception of the powers of God. Perhaps it is God.
5 Fred Hoyle, *The Black Cloud* (Harmondsworth, 1971), p. 163.
6 Peter Singer, *Animal Liberation*, Avon, 1977, and Peter Singer and Tom Regan, *Animal Rights and Human Obligation*, 1976 and Stanley and Rosalind Godlovitch, and J. Harris, *Animals, Men and Morals* (London, 1971).
7 For example witness the terrible fate of the Lycians of Xanthus as retold by Herodotus in the *Histories*, trans. Aubrey de Selincourt, (Harmondsworth, 1968), pp. 84 and 85.
8 The distinction between the respective value of needs and wants has been brilliantly drawn by Bob Dylan in 'Stuck inside of mobile with thee' on the album *Blonde on Blond*, CBS 66012, produced by Bob Johnson.

Chapter 2 A defence of non-'violent' violence

1 Hans Toch, *Violent Men* (1969; reprinted Harmondsworth, 1972).
2 See for example Joan V. Bondurant, *Conquest of Violence* (Princeton, 1958), for a discussion of this aspect of Gandhi's thought.
3 Examples of the Marxist conception of violence can be found *inter alia* in Frederick Engels, *The Condition of the Working Class in England*, trans. and ed. W. O. Henderson and W. H. Chaloner (Oxford, 1958), p. 108. and Christopher Caudwell, *Studies in a Dying Culture* (London, 1938), p. 102.

156

4 Johan Galtung, 'Violence, Peace and Peace Research', *Journal of Peace Research*, Autumn, 1969.
5 Newton Gerver, 'What Violence Is', in *Philosophy for a New Generation*, A. K. Bierman and James A. Gould (eds) (London, 1970).
6 Robert L. Holmes, 'Violence and Nonviolence', in *Violence*, Jerome A. Shaffer (ed.) (New York, 1971).
7 Sidney Hook, 'The Ideology of Violence', *Encounter*, April, 1970, p. 26.
8 Ted Honderich, 'Democratic Violence', *Philosophy and Public Affairs*, vol. 2, no. 2 Winter, 1973.
9 R. P. Wolff, 'On Violence', *Journal of Philosophy*, vol. 66, no. 19, October 1969.
10 Peter Mark Roget, *Thesaurus of English Words and Phrases* (Harmondsworth, 1954).
11 Charles Dickens, *Bleak House*, Chapter 32.
12 Morris Fraser, 'Children of Violence', *Sunday Times Weekly Review*, 29 April 1973, p. 33.
13 I do not mean here to beg the question of what is to count as a person against chimpanzees or dolphins or indeed against machines. All of these species have their champions but until much more evidence is gathered I will assume that none of these species are or contain persons.
14 W. Barrington-Moore Jr, *The Social Origins of Dictatorship and Democracy* (Harmondsworth, 1969), p. 103.
15 Ibid.
16 James Callaghan reported in *The Times*, 16 February 1970, commenting on what came to be known as the 'Garden House Affair'.
17 Sir Harold Wilson: a radio statement reported in *The Times*, 14 January 1971.
18 Sir Robert Mark interviewed by Michael Parkinson, BBC TV, 30 September 1978. The novelist Anthony Burgess who was another guest on the Parkinson programme heartily concurred with Sir Robert Mark's judgment.
19 See George Rudé, *The Crowd in History* (New York, 1964), and see also George Rudé, *The Crowd in the French Revolution* (Oxford, 1959).

Chapter 3 Negative actions

1 See Chapter 8.
2 Plutarch, *Life of Mark Antony*, trans. Ian Scott-Kilvert (Harmondsworth, 1965), p. 287.
3 Quoted in Norman Cohn, *The Pursuit of the Millennium* (London, 1957; reprinted 1970), p. 202.

4 Ibid.
5 Frederick Engels, *The Condition of the Working Class in England*, trans. and ed. W. O. Henderson and W. H. Chaloner (Oxford, 1958).
6 Ibid., p. 108.
7 Christopher Caudwell, *Studies in a Dying Culture* (London, 1938).
8 Ibid., p. 102.
9 Ibid., p. 116.
10 Harold Orlans, 'An American Death Camp' in B. Rosenberg, I. Gerver and F. W. Howton (eds), *Mass Society in Crisis: Social Problems and Social Pathology* (New York, 1964).
11 Ibid.
12 W. Barrington Moore, Jr, *The Social Origins of Dictatorship and Democracy* (Harmondsworth, 1969).
13 Ibid., p. 103.
14 Karl Marx, *Capital*, I, ed. F. Engels, trans. Samuel Moore and Edward Aveling (London, 1887; reprinted 1957). Chapter 15 sec. 8.c., pp. 466 ff.
15 Ibid., p. 480.
16 H. L. A. Hart and A. M. Honoré, *Causation in the Law* (Oxford, 1959).
17 Ibid., pp. 28, 29.
18 Jeremy Bentham, *Introduction to the Principles of Morals and Legislation*, ed. Wilfred Harrison (Oxford, 1967).
19 Ibid., Chapter 8, para. 8.
20 Eric D'Arcy, *Human Acts* (Oxford, 1963) pp. 47-9, 55.
21 Ibid., p. 49.
22 Ibid., p. 50.
23 John Casey, 'Actions and Consequences' in *Morality and Moral Reasoning*, ed. John Casey (London, 1971), p. 180.
24 Ibid., p. 187.
25 Ibid., p. 167.
26 Ibid., p. 182.
27 Ibid., p. 197.
28 Ibid., p. 205.
29 Barrington Moore Jr, *Social Origins*, p. 103.
30 Charles Dickens, *A Tale of Two Cities*, Book 2, Chapter 8.
31 Ludwig Wittgenstein, *Philosophical Investigations* (Oxford, 1963) Part II, S. XI.
32 See Chapter 7.
33 H. L. A. Hart and A. M. Honoré, *Causation in the Law*.
34 Ibid., p. 34.
35 Ibid., p. 35.
36 This is not perhaps the best example since it did not become clear that vaccination against smallpox was effective until the practice had become reasonably widespread. But with the modern practice of clinical trials we can easily imagine cases in which a completely new method of

preventing or curing disease might be developed and proved effective before its use was at all general, let alone a second nature.

37 There is further a problem about side-effects which emerge slowly. I will assume for simplicity that clinical trials allow for this. In cases in which, as a result of disasters like the thalidomide affair, use of a drug is restricted for many years so that possible side-effects can be spotted, we might have to postpone our causal attribution and then even abandon our attribution of responsibility.

38 Hart and Honoré, *Causation in the Law*, p. 33.

39 Ibid.

40 We will be examining all of these issues at closer quarters as the discussion progresses.

41 H. L. A. Hart, 'Postscript: Responsibility and Punishment', in *Punishment and Responsibility* (Oxford, 1968), pp. 212-30.

Chapter 4 Killing and letting die

1 Leonard Geddes, 'On the Intrinsic Wrongness of Killing Innocent People', *Analysis*, vol. 33, no. 3, January 1973.

2 In a private discussion.

3 R. A. Duff 'Absolute Principles and Double Effect', *Analysis*, vol. 36, January 1976.

4 Ibid., p. 74.

5 Ibid.

6 Ibid.

7 Ibid., p. 77.

8 William Shakespeare, *Richard III*, Act 1, Scene 2.

9 Duff, 'Absolute Principles', p. 68.

10 Ibid., p. 78.

11 Ibid., p. 79.

12 Jonathan Bennett, 'Whatever the Consequences', *Analysis*, vol. 26, no. 3, 1966.

13 Ibid., p. 94.

14 Daniel Dinello, 'On Killing and Letting Die', *Analysis*, vol. 31, no. 3, January 1971.

15 Ibid., p. 85.

16 Harold Orlans, 'An American Death Camp' in B. Rosenberg, I. Gerver and F. W. Howton (eds), *Mass Society in Crisis: Social Problems and Social Pathology* (New York, 1964).

17 Ibid.

18 Dwight MacDonald, 'Appendix to Orlans' in his *Mass Society in Crisis* (New York, 1964).

19 Ibid.

20 Phillippa Foot, 'The Problem of Abortion and Doctrine of the Double Effect', *Oxford Review* (Trinity, 1967). Mrs Foot amended her views on killing and letting die in a paper given in Oxford in 1976/7.

21 Mrs Foot is certainly right about the rights people have at present and Robert Nozick would agree with her (see his *Anarchy, State and Utopia* (Oxford, 1974)).

22 Ibid., p. 9.

23 See Chapter 5.

Chapter 5 The survival lottery

1 G. E. M. Anscombe, 'Who is wronged?', *Oxford Review* (Trinity, 1967), p. 16.

2 Ibid., p. 17.

3 Jonathan Glover, *Causing Death and Saving Lives* (Harmondsworth, 1977).

4 I have constructed this quotation from an earlier draft of Glover's book and from the final version, but see ibid., pp. 208, 209.

5 See P. J. FitzGerald, 'Acting and Refraining', *Analysis*, vol. 27, no. 4, March 1967.

6 Noam Chomsky, *American Power and the New Mandarins* (Harmondsworth, 1969), p. 11.

7 Stuart Hampshire, *Morality and Pessimism* (Cambridge, 1972).

8 Bernard Williams, 'A critique of Utilitarianism', in J. J. C. Smart and Bernard Williams, *Utilitarianism for and Against* (Cambridge, 1973).

9 Jonathan Bennett, 'The Conscience of Huckleberry Finn', *Philosophy*, vol. 49, no. 188, April 1974.

10 J. G. Hanink, 'On the Survival Lottery', *Philosophy*, vol. 51, no. 196, April, 1976, pp. 223-5.

11 Ibid., p. 225. And again 'intention' proves far too supple a notion to be of help.

12 In an otherwise sensitive treatment of this sort of problem Onora Nell seems to fall for something like the Hanink line; see 'Lifeboat Earth', *Philosophy and Public Affairs*, vol. 4, no. 3, Spring 1975, especially p. 281.

13 This is not strictly true of course since there is always some risk in surgical operations but, assuming as we have, that transplant procedures have been perfected, the risk would be small compared with the alternatives and can be disregarded for our present purposes.

14 For an interesting discussion of this question see Peter Singer, 'Utility and The Survival Lottery', *Philosophy*, no. 52, 1977.

15 There has been a vigorous debate on this point; see John M. Taurek, 'Should the Numbers Count?', *Philosophy and Public Affairs*, vol. 6,

no. 4, Summer 1977, and Derek Parfit, 'Innumerate Ethics', *Philosophy and Public Affairs*, vol. 7, no. 4, Summer 1978.

16 'Unhappy' for the argument.

17 Even those who feel they must reject the survival lottery at all costs in any of its versions, should be grateful for what they will see as a counter-example both to utilitarianism and to Rawls's theory of justice. The ways in which the survival lottery should be mandatory for utilitarians have already been considered. Rawlsians would accept it for a number of reasons: because it is rational in the Rawlsian sense; because it is fair; because, at the level of legislation, it improves the position of the least advantaged (the dying). It would, in short, clearly be chosen by people in the initial position.

Chapter 6 The fate of others and our distance from it

1 And this is not my experience alone. Alan Ryan who also put my 'survival lottery' to a number of people reports a similar reaction: Alan Ryan, 'Two Kinds of Morality', *New Society*, vol. 32, no. 652, p. 24, 3 April 1975.

2 British Transplantation Society, 'The Shortage of Organs for Clinical Transplantation: Document for Discussion', *British Medical Journal*, 1, 1975, 251-5.

3 Ibid., p. 251.

4 Ibid.

5 Ibid.

6 Roy Calne, 'Malaise of Clinical Organ Grafting', *Nature*, vol. 255, 1 May 1975. See also R. Y. Calne, 'The present position and future prospects of organ transplants', *Annals of Royal College of Surgeons*, 42, 1968, p. 283.

7 Ibid., pp. 291 ff. For a more pessimistic view see W. J. Dempster, 'Confused and Contradictory: The State of Transplantation', *World Medicine*, 9 April 1975.

8 British Transplantation Society, p. 253.

9 John Mahoney, SJ, *The Times*, 3 February 1975.

10 British Transplantation Society, p. 255.

11 Calne, 'Present position and future prospects of organ transplants', *Annals of the Royal College of Surgeons*, p. 291.

12 J. F. Pantridge 'Mobile Coronary Care Units' in J. R. Muir (ed.), *Prospects in the Management of Ischaemic Heart Disease*, CIBA Laboratories (Horsham, 1974). See also J. F, Pantridge 'Prehospital Coronary Care', *British Heart Journal* 36, 1974, 233-7.

13 L. A. Cobb and H. Alvares III, *Medic I: The Seattle System for Management of Out-of-Hospital Emergencies*. National Conference on

Emergency Cardiac Care, National Research Council and National Academy of Sciences, Washington DC, 1973.

14 Pantridge, 'Prehospital Coronary Care', p. 236.

15 *Medical Journal of Australia*, Editorial, 1 1975, 605. I do not know if the figures quoted were based on the Seattle figures or independently arrived at. It should also be noted that the provision of mobile units is not the only factor in the success of such units. Such provision must be accompanied by education of the public in the recognition of symptoms and the need for a quick call for medical help.

16 K. Astvad *et al.*, 'Mortality from Acute Myocardial Infarction Before and After Establishment of a Coronary Care Unit', *British Medical Journal* 1, 1974, 567-9.

17 Ibid.

18 J. A. Davis, letter in *British Medical Journal* 2, 1974, 333.

19 Ibid.

20 Ibid.

21 Jonathan Glover, *Causing Death and Saving Lives* (Harmondsworth, 1978).

22 Alan Ryan: talk on 'Personal View', BBC Radio 3, 31 January 1976.

23 Ibid.

24 F. W. Winterbotham, *The Ultra Secret* (London, 1974; reprinted 1975) pp. 83, 84. There are conflicting accounts of just how much warning Churchill had of the raid. See also Anthony Cave Brown *A Bodyguard of Lies* (London, 1976). For a different version of events see R. V. Jones, *Most Secret War* (London, 1979); chapter 18, p. 204.

25 See Carolyn R. Morillo's comment on the survival lottery: 'As Sure as Shooting, *Philosophy*, vol. 51, no. 195, January 1976, pp. 81, 82. I am indebted to Dr Morillo for a number of points of contact between the survival lottery and the military draft. See also her 'Doing, Refraining and the Strenuousness of Morality', *American Philosophical Quarterly*, 1977.

26 Morillo, 'As Sure as Shooting', p. 82.

27 See Chapter 3.

28 Morillo, 'As Sure as Shooting', p. 84.

29 Lawrence C. Becker, 'The Neglect of Virtue', *Ethics*, vol. 85, no. 2, January 1975.

30 Ibid., p. 118.

31 Ibid., p. 121.

32 Ibid.

33 Ibid., p. 122.

34 See Morillo, 'As Sure as Shooting', p. 85.

35 See Alan Ryan, 'Two Kinds of Morality', *New Society*, vol. 32, no. 652, April 1975 pp. 24 and 25 and, more generally, Mary Douglas, *Purity and Danger* (London, 1966).

36 William Shakespeare, *King Richard III, I. iv.*
37 Morillo, 'As Sure as Shooting', p. 85.
38 Chapter 5, 'Last Door Arguments'.
39 Becker, 'Neglect of Virtue', p. 118.
40 Ibid.
41 I am leaving aside questions such as the rights of the individuals concerned. Our belief in due process and so on. These might add up to a reason of sufficient moral weight to make the difference we want but if they seem to do so I think it's because of the point to which we are about to come.
42 The point of course is not that we must *individuate* the man who will benefit, but that we know that there is one who will for sure and certain benefit. As in the case where we cannot point out who our donations to famine relief will save but there is someone who will be saved.
43 When, for example, the evidence is that far from convincing populations that the price of continuing the struggle is too high, terror bombing only stiffens their resolve.
44 William Shakespeare, *Julius Caesar*, II. i. Whether in the light of the ensuing Civil War Brutus made the right decision is, of course, another matter but we should note that *he* hated tyranny more than he valued life.

Chapter 7 Integrity, sympathy and negative responsibility

 1 Bernard Williams, 'A Critique of Utilitarianism', in J. J. C. Smart and Bernard Williams, *Utilitarianism For and Against* (Cambridge, 1973).
 2 Utilitarianism is strictly speaking a type of consequentialism but for present purposes I use these terms interchangeably.
 3 Ibid., p. 95.
 4 Ibid., p. 116.
 5 Ibid., pp. 97 ff. In the original Pedro is the captain's hatchet-man but it simplifies the argument to ignore this unnecessary multiplication of murderers.
 6 Ibid., p. 118.
 7 Ibid., p. 108-9.
 8 Ibid., p. 118.
 9 Leo Tolstoy, *Anna Karenina*, trans. Rosemary Edmonds (Harmondsworth, 1954), p. 826.
10 George Orwell, letter to Humphrey House, 11 April, 1940 in *The Collected Essays, Journalism and Letters of George Orwell* vol. 1 (Harmondsworth, 1970), p. 583.
11 Noam Chomsky, *American Power and the New Mandarins* (Harmondsworth, 1969).

12 It is one of the ironies of civilisation that having swept the unfortunate out of sight we have to be made aware of their existence, and our sympathy aroused, through advertising.

13 Williams, 'Critique of Utilitarianism', p. 117.

14 See for example Bernard Williams, 'The Idea of Equality' in Peter Laslett and W. G. Runciman (eds) *Philosophy, Politics and Society* (Oxford, 1967; 2nd series), p. 114.

15 Jonathan Bennett 'The conscience of Huckleberry Finn', *Philosophy*, vol. 49, no. 188, April 1974.

16 Ibid., p. 133.

17 Ibid.

18 Ibid., p. 124.

19 Joseph Butler, *Fifteen Sermons Preached at the Rolls Chapel*, ed. T. A. Roberts (London, 1970), sermon 11. I am grateful to Alan Montefiore for pointing out to me the parallel between Butler's distinction and the point I wished to make.

20 See for example Ronald Dworkin's discussion of some of the necessary conditions of someone's holding a moral position in 'Lord Devlin and the Enforcement of Morals', *Yale Law Journal*, 76, 1966, pp. 986-1005.

21 Bennett, 'Conscience of Huckleberry Finn', p. 128.

22 Ibid., p. 127.

Chapter 8 Neutrality

1 Gaius Suetonius Tranquillus, *The Twelve Caesars*, trans. Robert Graves (Harmondsworth, 1957) p. 40.

2 Matthew 12:30.

3 Luke 10:50.

4 Leszek Kolakowski, 'Neutrality and academic values', in A. Montefiore (ed.), *Neutrality and Impartiality* (Cambridge, 1975).

5 Ibid., p. 77.

6 Montefiore, *Neutrality and Impartiality*.

7 Kolakowski, 'Neutrality and academic values', p. 72.

8 Hannah Arendt, *Eichmann in Jerusalem* (New York, 1963).

9 Ibid., p. 279.

10 Ibid.

11 See Chapter 2.

12 Montefiore, *Neutrality and Impartiality*, p. 11.

13 See Chapters 3 and 4.

14 See for example the argument of Chapter 4.

15 In Chapter 2.

16 Montefiore, *Neutrality and Impartiality*, p. 15.

17 Ronald Dworkin, 'The Right to Go to Law School', *New York Review*

of Books, vol. 23, no. 1, 5 February 1976.
18 Equality appears in both Montefiore's and Kolakowski's definitions.
In Montefiore's obviously because it involves equal help or hindrance
to all but also in Kolakowski's because non-involvement also amounts
to giving equal help or hindrance to all i.e. *Zero* help or hindrance to
all. There is an argument for the fundamental role of treatment as an
equal in the concept of neutrality in Dworkin's, 'The Right to Go to
Law School'.

Chapter 9 The bounds of obligation

1 'Neutralise' here means 'render ineffective', killing is I suppose the surest
method but the dead are not neutrals.
2 See Joel Feinberg, 'Collective Responsibility' in *Doing and Deserving*
(Princeton, 1970).
3 For example: Phillippa Foot, 'The Problem of Abortion and the
Doctrine of the Double Effect', *Oxford Review* (Trinity, 1967), p. 11,
and also Peter Singer, 'Famine, Affluence and Morality', *Philosophy
and Public Affairs*, vol. 3, no. 2, Winter 1974, p. 198.
4 R. M. Hare, 'Abortion and the Golden Rule', *Philosophy and Public
Affairs*, vol. 4, no. 3, Spring 1975.
5 Ibid., p. 215.
6 Ibid., p. 216.
7 Bernard Williams, 'A Critique of Utilitarianism' in J. J. C. Smart and
Bernard Williams, *Utilitarianism For and Against*, (Cambridge, 1973),
pp. 109, 110.
8 Ibid.
9 P. H. Nowell-Smith, *Ethics* (Harmondsworth, 1954; reprinted 1965),
p. 268.
10 Plato, *Protagoras*, trans. H. P. D. Lee (Harmondsworth, 1966).
11 Bertrand Russell, 'Is Happiness Still Possible' in *The Conquest of
Happiness* (London, 1930), p. 56.
12 F. M. Cornford, *Microcosmographia Academica* (London, 1966),
Chapters 7 and 8.

Bibliography

Anscombe, G. E. M., 'Who is wronged?', *Oxford Revue* (Trinity, 1967).

Arendt, Hannah, *Eichmann in Jerusalem* (New York, 1963).

Arendt, Hannah, *On Violence* (London, 1970).

Astvad, K. *et al.*, 'Mortality from Acute Myocardial Infarction Before and After Establishment of a Coronary Care Unit', *British Medical Journal*, 1, 1974, 567-9.

Barrington Moore Jr, W., *The Social Origins of Dictatorship and Democracy* (Harmondsworth, 1969).

Barrington Moore Jr, W., *Reflection on the causes of Human Misery* (London, 1972).

Becker, Lawrence C., 'The Neglect of Virtue', *Ethics*, vol. 85, no. 2, January 1975.

Bennett, Jonathan, 'Whatever the Consequences', *Analysis*, vol. 26, no. 3, 1966.

Bennett, Jonathan, 'The Conscience of Huckleberry Finn', *Philosophy*, vol. 49, no. 188, April 1974.

Bentham, Jeremy, *Introduction to the Principles of Morals and Legislation*, ed., Wilfred Harrison (Oxford, 1967).

Bettleheim, Bruno, *The Informed Heart* (London, 1970).

Bienen, Henry, *Violence and Social Change* (London, 1968).

Bondurant, Joan V., *Conquest of Violence* (Princeton, 1958).

Brown, R. M. (ed.), *American Violence* (New York, 1970).

British Transplantation Society, 'The Shortage of Organs for Clinical Transplantation: Document for Discussion', *British Medical Journal*, 1975, 1, pp. 251-5.

Butler, Joseph, *Fifteen Sermons Preached at the Rolls Chapel*, ed. T. A. Roberts (London, 1970), Sermon 11.

Calne, Roy, 'Malaise of Clinical Organ Grafting', *Nature*, vol. 255, 1 May 1975.

Calne, Roy, in 'The present position and future prospects of organ transplantation' in *Annals of Royal College of Surgeons*, 1968, 42. 283.

Cave Brown, Anthony, *A Bodyguard of Lies* (London, 1976).

Casey, John, 'Actions and Consequences' in *Morality and Moral Reasoning* ed. John Casey (London, 1971).

Caudwell, Christopher, *Studies in a Dying Culture* (London, 1938).

Chomsky, Noam, *American Power and the New Mandarins* (Harmondsworth, 1969).

Cobb, L. A. and Alvarez, H. III, *Medic I: The Seattle System for Management of out-of-hospital Emergencies*, National Conference of Emergency Cardiac Care National Research Council and National Academy of Sciences, Washington DC, 1973.

Cohn, Norman, *The Pursuit of the Millennium* (London, 1957; reprinted 1970).

Cornford, F. M., *Microcosmographia Academica* (London, 1966).

D'Arcy, Eric, *Human Acts* (Oxford, 1963).

Davis, J. A., letter in *British Medical Journal*, 2, 1974, p. 333.

Dempster, W. J., 'Confused and Contradictory: The State of Transplantation', *World Medicine*, 9 April 1975.

Dickens, Charles, *Bleak House* (London, 1966).

Dinello, Daniel, 'On Killing and Letting Die', *Analysis*, vol. 31, no. 3, January 1971.

Douglas, Mary, *Purity and Danger* (London, 1966).

Duff, R. A., 'Absolute Principles and Double Effect', *Analysis*, vol. 36, January 1976.

Dworkin, Ronald, 'Lord Devlin and the Enforcement of Morals', *Yale Law Journal* 76, 1966, pp. 986-1005.

Dworkin, Ronald, 'The Right to Go to Law School', *New York Review of Books*, vol. 23, no. 1, 5 February 1976.

Dworkin, Ronald, *Taking Rights Seriously* (London, 1977).

Engels, Frederick, *The Condition of the Working Class in England*, trans. and ed. W. O. Henderson and W. H. Chaloner (Oxford, 1958).

Feinberg, Joel, 'Collective Responsibility' in *Doing and Deserving* (Princeton, 1970).

Feinberg, Joel, 'Voluntary Euthanasia and the Unalienable Right to Life', *Philosophy and Public Affairs*, vol. 7, no. 2, Winter 1978.

FitzGerald, P. J., 'Acting and Refraining', *Analysis*, vol. 27, no. 4, March 1967.

Foot, Phillippa, 'The Problem of Abortion and the Doctrine of the Double Effect', *Oxford Review* (Trinity, 1967).

Foot, Phillippa, 'Euthanasia', *Philosophy and Public Affairs*, vol. 6, no. 2, Winter 1977.

Fraser, Morris, 'Children of Violence', *Sunday Times Weekly Review*, 29 April 1973.

Galtung, Johan, 'Violence, Peace and Peace Research', *Journal of Peace Research*, Autumn 1969.

Geddes, Leonard, 'On the Intrinsic Wrongness of Killing Innocent

People', *Analysis*, vol. 33, no. 3, January 1973.

Gerver, Newton, 'What Violence Is' in *Philosophy for a New Generation*, ed. A. K. Bierman and James A. Gould (London, 1970).

Glover, Jonathan, 'It makes no difference whether or not I do it', *Proceedings of the Aristotelian Society*, supp. vol. 1975.

Glover, Jonathan, *Causing Death and Saving Lives* (Harmondsworth, 1978).

Godlovitch, S. and R. and Harris, J., *Animals, Men and Morals* (London, 1971).

Hampshire, Stuart, *Morality and Pessimism* (Cambridge, 1972).

Hanink, J. G. 'On the Survival Lottery', *Philosophy*, vol. 51, no. 196, April 1976.

Hare, R. M., 'Abortion and the Golden Rule', *Philosophy and Public Affairs*, vol. 4, no. 3, Spring 1975.

Hart, H. L. A., 'Postscript: Responsibility and Punishment' in *Punishment and Responsibility* (Oxford, 1968).

Hart, H. L. A., *Punishment and Responsibility* (Oxford, 1968).

Hart, H. L. A. and Honoré, A. M., *Causation in the Law* (Oxford, 1959).

Holmes, Robert L., 'Violence and Nonviolence', *Violence*, ed. Jerome A. Shaffer (New York, 1971).

Honderich, Ted, 'Democratic Violence', *Philosophy and Public Affairs*, vol. 2, no. 2, Winter 1973.

Honderich, Ted, *Political Violence* (Cornell, 1977).

Hook, Sidney, 'The Ideology of Violence', *Encounter*, April 1970.

Kipnis, Kenneth (ed.) *Philosophical Issues in Law* (Englewood Cliffs, 1977).

Kleinig, John, 'Good Samaritanism', *Philosophy and Public Affairs*, vol. 5, no. 4, Summer 1976.

Kolakowski, Leszek, 'Neutrality and Academic Values' in A. Montefiore (ed.) *Neutrality and Impartiality* (Cambridge, 1975).

MacDonald, Dwight, 'Appendix to Orlans' in his *Mass Society in Crisis* (New York, 1964).

MacFarlane, Leslie, *Violence and the State* (London, 1974).

Marx, Karl, *Capital*, vol. 1, ed. F. Engels, trans. Samuel Moore and Edward Aveling (London, 1887; reprinted 1957).

Medical Journal of Australia, editorial 1975, 1, p. 604.

Montefiore, A. (ed.), *Neutrality and Impartiality* (Cambridge, 1975).

Morillo, Carolyn R., 'As Sure as Shooting', *Philosophy*, vol. 51, no. 195, January 1976.

Morillo, Carolyn R., 'Doing, Refraining and the strenuousness of Morality', *American Philosophical Quarterly*, 1977.

Nell, Onora, 'Lifeboat Earth', *Philosophy and Public Affairs*, vol. 4, no. 3, Spring 1975.

Nowell-Smith, P. H., *Ethics* (Harmondsworth, 1954; reprinted 1965).

Nozick, Robert, *Anarchy, State and Utopia* (Oxford, 1974).

Orlans, Harold, 'An American Death Camp' in B. Rosenberg, I. Gerver and F. W. Howton (eds), *Mass Society in Crisis: Social Problems and Social Pathology* (New York, 1964).

Orwell, George, letter to Humphrey House, 11 April 1940 in *The Collected Essays, Journalism and Letters of George Orwell*, vol. 1 (Harmondsworth, 1970).

Pantridge, J. F. 'Mobile Coronary Care Units' in J. R. Muir (ed.), *Prospects in the Management of Ischaemic Heart Disease*, CIBA Laboratories (Horsham, 1974).

Pantridge, J. F., 'Prehospital Coronary Care', *British Heart Journal*, 36, 1974, pp. 233-7.

Parfit, Derek, 'Innumerate Ethics', *Philosophy and Public Affairs*, vol. 7, no. 4, Summer 1978.

Plato, *Protagoras*, trans. H. P. D. Lee (Harmondsworth, 1966).

Plutarch, *Life of Mark Antony*, trans. Ian Scott-Kilvert (Harmondsworth, 1965).

Rawls, John, *A Theory of Justice* (Cambridge, Mass., 1971).

Roget, Peter Mark, *Thesaurus of English Words and Phrases* (Harmondsworth, 1954).

Roupas, T. G., 'The Value of Life', *Philosophy and Public Affairs*, vol. 7, no. 2, Winter 1978.

Rudé, George, *The Crowd in the French Revolution* (Oxford, 1959).

Rudé, George, *The Crowd in History* (New York, 1964).

Russell, Bertrand, 'Is Happiness Still Possible' in *The Conquest of Happiness* (London, 1930), p. 56.

Russell, Bruce, 'On the Relative Strictness of Negative and Positive Duties', *American Philosophical Quarterly*, vol. 14, no. 2, April 1977.

Ryan, Alan, 'Two Kinds of Morality', *New Society*, vol. 32, no. 652, 3 April 1975.

Shaffer, J. A. (ed.), *Violence* (New York, 1971).

Singer, Peter, 'Famine, Affluence and Morality', *Philosophy and Public Affairs*, vol. 3, no. 2, Winter 1974.

Singer, Peter, 'Utility and the Survival Lottery', *Philosophy*, no. 52, 1977.

Suetonius, Gaius Tranquillus, *The Twelve Caesars*, trans. Robert Graves (Harmondsworth, 1957).

Taurek, John M., 'Should the Numbers Count?', *Philosophy and Public Affairs*, vol. 6, no. 4, Summer 1977.

Thompson, E. P., *The Making of the English Working Class* (London, 1963).

Thompson, E. P., *The Poverty of Theory and Other Essays* (London, 1978).

Thomson, Judith Jarvis, 'A Defence of Abortion', *Philosophy and Public Affairs*, vol. 1, no. 1, Fall 1971.

Toch, Hans, *Violent Men* (1969; reprinted Harmondsworth, 1972).

Tolstoy, Leo, *Anna Karenina*, trans. Rosemary Edmonds (Harmondsworth, 1954).

Tooley, Michael, 'Abortion and Infanticide', *Philosophy and Public Affairs*, vol. 2, no. 1, Fall 1972.

Trammell, R. L., 'Tooley's Moral Symmetry Principle', *Philosophy and Public Affairs*, vol. 5, no. 3, Spring 1976.

Williams, Bernard, 'A Critique of Utilitarianism' in J. J. C. Smart and Bernard Williams, *Utilitarianism For and Against* (Cambridge 1973).

Williams, Bernard, 'The Idea of Equality' in Peter Laslett and W. G. Runciman (eds), *Philosophy, Politics and Society*, (Oxford, 1967; 2nd series).

Winterbotham, F. W., *The Ultra Secret* (London, 1974; reprinted 1975), pp. 83, 84.

Wittgenstein, Ludwig, *Philosophical Investigations* (Oxford, 1963).

Wittgenstein, Ludwig, 'A Lecture on Ethics', *Philosophical Review*, 74, 1965.

Wolff, R. P., 'On Violence', *The Journal of Philosophy*, vol. 66, no. 19, 2 October 1969.

Wolff, R. P., 'Beyond Tolerance' in R. P. Wolff, W. Barrington Moore Jr, and Herbert Marcuse, *A Critique of Pure Tolerance* (Boston, 1969).

Select bibliography

Violence

Anscombe, Elizabeth, 'War and Murder', in W. Stein, *Nuclear Weapons a Catholic Response* (London, 1963).

Arendt, Hannah, *On Violence* (London, 1970).

Arendt, Hannah, *Eichmann in Jerusalem* (New York, 1963).

Barrington Moore Jr, W., *The Social Origins of Dictatorship and Democracy* (Harmondsworth, 1967).

Barrington Moore Jr, W., *Reflections On the Causes of Human Misery* (London, 1972).

Bay, Christian, 'Violence as a Negation of Freedom', *American Scholar*, Autumn 1971.

Bienen, Henry, *Violence and Social Change* (London, 1968).

Bondurant, Joan V., *Conquest of Violence* (Princeton, 1958).

Brown, R. M. (ed.), *American Violence* (New York, 1970).

Brown, Claude, *Manchild in the Promised Land* (Harmondsworth, 1969).

Brown, H. Rap, *Die Nigger Die* (London 1969).

Cameron, J. M., 'The Ethics of Violence', *New York Review of Books*, 2 July 1970.

Caudwell, Christopher, *Studies in a Dying Culture* (London, 1938).

Cleaver, Eldridge, *Post Prison Writings and Speeches* (London, 1969).

Cleaver, Eldridge, *Soul on Ice* (London, 1969).

Cohn, Norman, *The Pursuit of the Millennium* (London, 1970).

Engels, Frederich, *The Condition of the Working Class in England*, trans. and ed. W. O. Henderson and W. H. Chaloner (Oxford, 1958).

Fanon, Frantz, *The Wretched of the Earth* (Harmondsworth, 1967).

Fanon, Frantz, *Black Skin, White Masks* (London, 1970).

Fraser, Morris, 'Children of Violence', *Sunday Times Weekly Review*, 29 April 1973.

Galtung, Johan, 'Violence, Peace and Peace Research', *Journal of Peace Research*, Autumn 1969.

Gerver, Newton, 'What Violence Is' in *Philosophy for a New Generation* ed. A. K. Bierman and James A. Gould (London, 1970).

Gray, J. Glenn, *On Understanding Violence Philosophically* (New York, 1970).

Honderich, Ted, 'Democratic Violence', *Philosophy and Public Affairs*, vol. 2, no. 2, Winter 1973.

Hook, Sidney, 'The Ideology of Violence', *Encounter*, April 1970.

Hook, Sidney, 'Rights of Victims', *Encounter*, April 1972.

Jones, R. V., *Most Secret War* (London, 1979).

Lawrence, John, 'Violence', *Social Theory and Practice*, vol. 1, no. 2, Fall 1970.

Lorenz, Konrad, *On Aggression* (London, 1963).

Macfarlane, Leslie, *Violence and The State* (London, 1974).

Mailer, Norman, *The White Negro*, (San Francisco, 1957).

Ryan, Alan, 'Views', *Listener*, 30 December 1971.

Seale, Bobby, *Seize The Time* (London, 1970).

Shaffer, P. (ed.), *Violence* (New York, 1971).

Singer, Peter, *Democracy and Disobedience* (London, 1973).

Storr, Anthony, *Human Aggression* (London, 1968).

Storr, Anthony, *Human Destructiveness* (London, 1972).

Szasz, Thomas S., *The Manufacture of Madness* (London, 1971).

Vanden Haag, Ernest, *Political Violence and Civil Disobedience* (New York, 1972).

Wade, Francis C., 'On Violence', *Journal of Philosophy*, 1971.

Weber, Max, 'Politics as a Vocation' in H. H. Gerth and C. Wright Mills, *From Max Weber* (London, 1967).

Weil, Simone, 'The Illiad, A Poem of Force' in Peter Meyer, (ed.) *The Pacifist Conscience* (London, 1966).

Wolff, R. P., 'On Violence', *Journal of Philosophy*, vol. 66, no. 19, October 1969.

Wolin, Sheldon, S., 'Violence and The Western Political Tradition', *American Journal of Orthopsychiatry*, vol. 33, 1962.

Zinn, Howard, *Disobedience and Democracy* (New York, 1968).

Positive and negative acts

Barrington Moore Jr., W., *The Social Origins of Dictatorship and Democracy* (Harmondsworth, 1969).

Becker, Lawrence, C., 'The Neglect of Virtue', *Ethics*, vol. 85, no. 2, January 1975.

Bennett, Jonathan, 'Whatever the Consequences', *Analysis*, vol. 26, no. 3, 1966.

Bentham, Jeremy, *Introduction to the Principles of Morals and Legislation*, (ed.) Wilfred Harrison (Oxford, 1974).

Casey, John, 'Action and Consequences' in *Morality and Moral Reason-*

ing, ed. John Casey (London, 1971).

D'Arcy, Eric, *Human Acts* (Oxford, 1963).

Dinello, Daniel, 'On Killing and Letting Die', *Analysis*, vol. 31, January 1971.

Duff, R. A., 'Absolute Principles and Double Effect', *Analysis*, January 1976.

Finnis, John, 'The Rights and Wrongs of Abortion: A Reply to Judith Thomas', *Philosophy and Public Affairs*, 1973.

Fitzgerald, P. J., 'Acting and Refraining', *Analysis*, vol. 27, 1967.

Foot, Phillippa, 'The Problem of Abortion and the Doctrine of the Double Effect', *Oxford Review* (Trinity, 1967).

Geddes, Leonard, 'On the Intrinsic Wrongness of Killing Innocent People', *Analysis*, vol. 33, no. 3, January 1973.

Glover, Jonathan, *Causing Death and Saving Lives* (Harmondsworth, 1977).

Hanink, J. G., 'Some Light on Double Effect', *Analysis*, 1975.

Hanink, J. G., 'On the Survival Lottery', *Philosophy*, vol. 51, no. 196, April 1976.

Hare, R. M., 'Abortion and The Golden Rule', *Philosophy and Public Affairs*, vol. 4, no. 3, Spring 1975.

Hart, H. L. A. and Honoré, A. M., *Causation in the Law* (Oxford, 1959).

Morillo, Carolyn R., 'As Sure As Shooting', *Philosophy*, January 1976.

Morillo, Carolyn R., 'Doing, Refraining and the Strenuousness of Morality', *American Philosophical Quarterly*, 1977.

Nell, Onora, 'Lifeboat Earth', *Philosophy and Public Affairs*, vol. 4, no. 3, Spring 1975.

Rachels, James, 'Active and Passive Euthanasia', *New England Journal of Medicine*, January 1975.

Ratcliffe, James, J., (ed.), *The Good Samaritan and the Law* (New York, 1966).

Russell, Bruce, 'On the Relative Strictness of Negative and Positive Duties', *American Philosophical Quarterly,* vol. 14, no. 2, April 1977.

Russell, Bruce, 'Still a Live Issue', *Philosophy and Public Affairs*, vol. 7, no. 3, Spring 1978.

Singer, Peter, 'Famine, Affluence and Morality', *Philosophy and Public Affairs*, 1972.

Smart, J. J. C. and Williams, Bernard, *Utilitarianism: For and Against* (Cambridge, 1973).

Thomson, Judith Jarvis, 'A Defence of Abortion', *Philosophy and Public Affairs*, vol. 1, no. 1, Fall 1971.

Thomson, Judith Jarvis, 'Rights and Deaths', *Philosophy and Public Affairs*, 1973.

Tooley, Michael, 'Abortion and Infanticide', *Philosophy and Public Affairs*, vol. 2, no. 1, Fall 1972.

Trammell, R. L., 'Saving and Taking Life', *Journal of Philosophy*, 1975.

Trammell, R. L., 'Tooley's Moral Symmetry Principle', *Philosophy and Public Affairs*, vol. 5, no. 3, Spring 1976.

Walzer, Michael, 'Political Action, The Problem of Dirty Hands', *Philosophy and Public Affairs*, 1973.

Index

175